Mastery

Mastery

A UNIVERSITY WORD LIST READER

Gladys Valcourt *and*
Linda Wells

Ann Arbor

THE UNIVERSITY OF MICHIGAN PRESS

To Virginia R. Valcourt Augustitus
in loving memory

Acknowledgments

Many thanks to everyone who helped with this book. We'd especially like to thank our editor, Kelly Sippell, for her enthusiasm, patience, and guidance in helping us turn our ideas into print. Our gratitude and thanks also to Mary Fore, illustrator, for her excellent portraits of our subjects; Paul Nation, Rod Ellis, Anita Sökmen, and Joan Barth for their ideas, constructive feedback, and support; Daphne Mackey, Lisa Carscadden, and special programs teachers at the University of Washington for testing units in their courses; and many other colleagues and students at the University of Washington, Temple University, and Temple University Japan for their generous assistance with this book. We appreciate all you have done.

Contents

Contents / xi

Introduction

Mastery, an academic reader built around the achievements of renowned Americans, introduces English as a second language students to the University Word List (UWL). The approximately eight hundred high-frequency words on this list, developed by Xue Guoyi and Paul Nation 9in 1984, are the English words most widely used in academic settings, that is, those that occur frequently across many disciplines. Adding the words from this list to a basic English vocabulary of two thousand words will enable ESL learners to understand about 95 percent of the vocabulary they encounter in their academic reading.

Theoretical Perspective

Reflecting the influence of psycholinguistic top-down approaches to reading, vocabulary instruction for the past two decades has emphasized the *implicit, incidental learning of words.* The focus has been on directing students to use the least number of cues to arrive at meaning and to infer from context whenever possible. New research findings suggest, however, that combining this top-down approach with strong *explicit, bottom-up skills* results in increased vocabulary gains. Currently, the recommended model for vocabulary instruction is an *interactive approach* that directs students not only to infer from context but also to incorporate new words within existing schemata, experience repeated encounters with the words, engage in deeper levels of processing, and use a variety of strategies for learning and retaining words. It is this current model that serves as the theoretical framework for *Mastery*.

Mastery assumes that academic vocabulary is best learned when students engage in two general kinds of activities: activities aimed at using words *accurately* and activities aimed at using words *fluently*. For this reason, the units of study include both form-focused and meaning-focused vocabulary instruction. *Form-focused instruction* attends to word parts, word relationships, word origins, collocations, word meaning, and the grammar of words. *Meaning-focused instruction* attends to the communicative uses of language: listening to what a friend has to say, talking about a work of art, reading about an interesting person, or writing a report for a course.

The *listening activities* in *Mastery* consist of listening to and working with authentic audio-taped biographical texts. Transcripts of these texts are provided in the teacher's manual. *Speaking activities* call for students to practice formulaic dialogues, engage in natural conversations, and give formal oral presentations. *Reading activities* are a key feature of the text. Reading these biographical selections provides students with a great deal of input about how the target vocabulary is commonly used in English. Additionally, the readings familiarize students with many aspects of American culture. Students read about Americans involved in business, social activism, sports, architecture, the arts, and many other areas of American life. This will help students to develop not only language skills but also a better understanding of American culture. A wide variety of *writing exercises*, ranging from creative writing to writing for a particular discourse community, is also included in *Mastery*.

The theoretical framework underlying *Mastery* emphasizes studying words separately as distinct language items and also learning them, in natural contexts, as part of a language system that is used to communicate effectively with others.

Organization

Mastery consists of twelve units, each with readings about fifteen hundred words long. Nine of the units introduce new vocabulary; three review units recycle words already studied. The units are presented according to graded levels of reading difficulty, with earlier units being easier than later ones.

Mastery is a user-friendly text that contains a number of features to facilitate student learning and teacher instruction. These include glossed words and phrases, easily scored review tests, and three appendixes: the University Word List, the Answer Key, and instructions on how to make vocabulary index cards.

Suggestions for the Self-Study Student

Mastery can be used for self-study by learners who are not enrolled in an ESL program but who want to improve their vocabulary on their own. If you are one of these learners, here are some suggestions for using the text.

1. Find out how much you already know by completing the Vocabulary Preview (at the beginning of each unit) and the Review sections of the text.
2. Go over the list of words in the Word Study section of the unit and cross out those that you already know.
3. Locate the remaining words in the reading passage and see if, from the context, you can guess what the words mean.
4. Consult your dictionary for the meanings of words you do not know. Write these in a vocabulary notebook. By the time you finish the notebook, you will have your own academic learner dictionary.
5. Work your way through the Vocabulary Preview and the reading selections of the unit. Check your dictionary for words not listed on your vocabulary list that are essential to your understanding of the reading.
6. As you read, check for comprehension by asking yourself periodically: Did I understand what I just read? Which sentence is giving me a problem? Why? What or who can help me understand this?
7. Also, as you are reading, stop to predict what is coming next. Is the reading passage going to give more details about an idea already presented? Is a new idea going to be presented?
8. Find a friend or a tutor who can help you with the communicative activities—someone who will listen to you and talk with you. Literacy councils and local libraries have volunteer tutors who can

help. Or, check with the international student center in your university. These centers often have tutors to help ESL students with their English.

9. Scan the Word Study section of the unit and complete those activities that you think might help you learn. Skip those that seem too easy for you. The listening exercises, as well as the vocabulary words and one of the readings from each unit (which may differ slightly from the text in your book), are on the *Mastery* audiotape. They are marked with this symbol 🎧.

10. When you have finished all of the activities you selected, turn to the Answer Key and check your answers.

11. Reread the reading selection to find out if the reading has become much easier to understand.

12. Use supplementary materials such as books, magazine articles, and videos to expand your knowledge of the topic. The web page for *Biography* on the Internet (http://www.biography.com), for example, advertises videos for Lee Iacocca, the Mustang, Gloria Steinem, and Maya Angelou.

Working your way through *Mastery* will help you to *master* the words needed for successful academic achievement. It will also enrich your understanding of the people and culture of the United States.

New York City

Washington, D.C.

Pittsburgh,
Pennsylvania

Detroit,
Michigan

Toledo, Ohio

Tuskegee,
Alabama

Montgomery,
Alabama

Stamps,
Arkansas

Abiquiu, New Mexico

Los Angeles,
California

Puerto Rico

Locations referred to in readings

Unit 1
Lee Iacocca

Vocabulary Preview

Preview 1

The following sentences contain information that appears in the reading on Lee Iacocca. Complete each one with the most suitable word.

features   research   options   consumers   economy

1. The Falcon was a very popular _____ car of the fifties.

2. After the war, _____ began to consider more sporty car models.

3. "We went back to the _____," said Iacocca, "to learn more about the changing car market."

4. Any car that would appeal to young customers would have to have three main _____: great styling, strong performance, and a low price.

5. Rather than develop different versions of the same car, the company decided to develop one car with many _____.

Preview 2

Look at the way the underlined words are used in the sentences. Match each word with its definition by writing the letter of the correct definition on the line.

1. According to Jung, human beings generally try to adapt to the demands of society.
2. "Water supply" refers to how much water is available to meet a need.
3. At public functions, a king often wears his ceremonial robes.
4. One of Canada's most valuable resources is its huge forests.
5. To be truly automatic, a machine must be capable of functioning without the assistance of an operator.

__ 1. adapt   a. big, enormous
__ 2. available   b. mechanical, self-acting

___ 3. function   c. adjust, fit in

___ 4. huge   d. present, at hand, obtainable

___ 5. automatic   e. formal gathering or celebration

Reading Preview: What Do You Know about Lee Iacocca?

Circle the correct answer. If you don't know the answer, guess.

1. Lee Iacocca is
   a. the president of the General Motors car company
   b. the president of a well-known computer software business
   c. the father of the Mustang
   d. the chief executive officer of Microsoft

2. The city in Michigan where most cars are made is
   a. Pontiac
   b. Detroit
   c. Ann Arbor
   d. East Lansing

3. All of the following are American car manufacturers except for
   a. Honda
   b. General Motors
   c. Chrysler
   d. Ford

Adapted from *Iacocca: An Autobiography* by Lee Iacocca with William Novak (New York: Bantam Doubleday Dell, 1984), 64–74.

Introduction to the Reading

Lee Iacocca is an American automobile executive who became famous in the early 1980s for being awarded the largest amount of federal aid ever given to a private corporation.

Iacocca was born in Allentown, Pennsylvania, in 1924. In 1946, after graduating from Princeton University with a degree in engineering, he went to work for the Ford Corporation. At Ford, Iacocca quickly established that he was better at sales than engineering. He worked hard on development and production, and by 1960, he was a vice president in the company. In the 1960s, Iacocca became famous for his leading role in the development and marketing of the **Mustang,** a sporty car developed by Ford that captured the heart of America as no other car had for a very long time.

After being dismissed by Ford in 1978 for his unusual way of doing things, Iacocca accepted the position of chairman of the board of the Chrysler Corporation. At that time, Chrysler was facing bankruptcy. The country was living through a serious oil crisis, and no one wanted to buy any of the many **gas-guzzling** luxury cars the company had in stock. Iacocca asked the federal government for financial aid, and he got it. The company was guaranteed $1.5 billion in loans. The move **paid off.** Four years later Chrysler announced record profits of more than $2.4 billion. Since then, Iacocca has been a national celebrity. The following reading, adapted from Iacocca's autobiography, *Iacocca*, tells about another great Iacocca achievement, the development of the Mustang.

mustang: a small wild horse found in the American West. **Mustang** was the name chosen by the Ford Motor Company for the very popular car it developed in the 1960s.
gas-guzzling: slang for a car that uses a lot of gas, that is not fuel efficient
paid off: worked, was successful

Reading: The Mustang

The 1964 Ford Mustang. Photo compliments of Ford Division Public Affairs, Detroit, MI. Reprinted with permission.

(1)   In the early 1960s, our **public relations department** began to get a lot of letters from people who wanted us to produce another **Thunderbird**. This was a surprise to us, because that car had not been very successful. But the mail was telling us consumer tastes were changing. Maybe the Thunderbird was simply ahead of its time, we said to ourselves. We were starting to get the impression that if the car were still on the market, it would be selling well.

(2)   At the same time, our market researchers were telling us that the youthful image of the new decade actually existed. For one thing, the average age of the population was falling at a rapid rate. The teenagers born in the **baby boom** that followed World War II were becoming adult consumers. The

public relations department: the office that advertises the company's product on radio, on television, and in other media in order to encourage consumers to buy it
Thunderbird: a sporty car manufactured by the Ford Motor Company in the 1950s
baby boom: a significant increase in the birthrate during a particular period of time, such as the period following World War II

twenty- to twenty-four-year-old group would increase by over 50 percent in the 1960s. Moreover, young adults between eighteen and thirty-four would **account for** at least half of the huge increase in car sales during the next ten years.

(3)   There were equally interesting changes going on among older car buyers. We were now starting to see buyers move away from the **economy cars** of the late 1950s that had helped the **Falcon** set new records. Consumers were beginning to look beyond the plain and the purely functional to consider more sporty and more luxurious models.

(4)   When we analyzed this information we concluded that while the **Edsel** had been a car in search of a market it never found, here was a market in search of a car. Normally Detroit carmakers built a new car and then tried to identify its buyers. But we were in a position to develop a new car specifically for a hungry new market.

(5)   Any car that would appeal to these young customers had to have three main features: great styling, strong performance, and a low price. Developing a new model with all three would not be easy. But if it could be done, we **had a shot at** major success.

(6)   We went back to the research to learn more about the changing market. First, there was enormous growth in families, with the second car typically smaller and more sporty than the first. Second, a growing number of cars were being bought by women, who preferred small cars with easy handling. Single people, too, were also among new car buyers, and they were choosing smaller and sportier models than their married friends. It was also clear that in the next few years, Americans would have more money than ever before to spend on transportation and entertainment.

(7)   The more our group talked, the more definite our ideas became. Our car had to be sporty and beautifully styled with just a touch of **nostalgia.** It had to be easy to identify and unlike anything else on the market. It had to be simple to operate but still capable of seating four people, with enough room left for a good-sized trunk. It had to be a sports car but more than a sports car. We wanted to develop a car that you could drive to the country club on Friday night, to the shopping center on Saturday, and to church on Sunday.

account for: explain the cause of
economy car: one that is cheap, that costs very little to run
Falcon: an economy car manufactured by the Ford Company in the 1950s
Edsel: a car manufactured by Ford that turned out to be very unsuccessful
had a shot at: had a chance for
nostalgia: remembrance, longing for the past

(8)   In sum, our intention was to appeal to several markets at once. We had to attract many different kinds of customers because the only way we could afford to make this car at a great price was **to sell a ton of them**. Rather than offer several different versions of the same car, we decided to develop one basic car with many options. That way the customer could buy as much economy, luxury, or performance as he wanted—or could afford.

(9)   But the question was: could we afford the car? An all-new car would cost $300 to $400 million. The answer lay in using available components. That way we could save a lot of money on production costs. The car parts for the Falcon already existed, so if we could adapt them, we wouldn't have **to start from scratch.** We could build the new car with the old parts of the Falcon and save a fortune. In the end we were able to develop the new car for only $75 million.

(10)   On March 9, 1964, the first Mustang rolled off the assembly line. It was a huge success. During the first week it was on sale, four million people visited Ford showrooms. People liked the car much more than we had expected.

(11)   It became immediately clear to me that we had to open up a second manufacturing plant. We had initially thought that the Mustang would sell seventy-five thousand units during the first year. But the projections kept growing, and before the car was even out, we were planning on sales of two hundred thousand. To build that many cars we had to talk top management into converting a second plant, in California, into producing more Mustangs.

(12)   People were buying Mustangs in record numbers. The options were moving just as quickly. Our customers reacted to the options like starving people react to food. Over 80 percent ordered **white sidewall tires**, 80 percent wanted radios, 71 percent chose eight cylinder engines, and 50 percent ordered the automatic transmission. For a car that cost $2,368, our customers were spending an average of $1,000 each just on options.

(13)   I had a target in mind for the first year. During its first year, the Falcon had sold a record 417,174 cars, and that was the figure I wanted to beat. We had a slogan: "417 by 4/17"—the Mustang's birthday. Late in the evening of April 16, 1965, a young Californian bought a sporty red Mustang convertible. He had just bought the 418,812th Mustang, and we finished our first year with a new record.

---

to sell a ton of them: to sell a huge number of Mustangs
to start from scratch: to start from the very beginning, to use all new parts
white sidewall tire: a tire decorated with a sporty white stripe on the side

(14)   The accountants, who had predicted the project was headed for failure, finally admitted that there was more than one way to build a car. It was the styling that did it, which was something they hadn't counted on. But they weren't shy when it came time to count the money. In the first two years alone, the Mustang earned **net profits** of $1.1 billion!

Comprehension Check

Check your understanding of the reading selection by marking these sentences true (*T*) or false (*F*).

— 1. The Mustang was the most popular economy car built in the 1960s by the Ford Corporation.

— 2. Lee Iacocca played a major role in developing the Mustang.

— 3. Like the Edsel, the Mustang was also very popular with consumers.

— 4. Researchers confirmed that, in the coming decade, Americans would be able to afford more expensive cars.

— 5. In order to appeal to several markets at once, Iacocca decided to design several versions of the Mustang.

— 6. The Ford Corporation saved on making the Mustang by using car components already available.

— 7. The first Mustang rolled off the assembly line on April 16, 1965.

— 8. The most popular option for the early Mustang was the automatic transmission.

— 9. The initial sales projections for the Mustang were too low.

— 10. The Mustang proved to be extremely popular because of three major features: great design, price, and all-around great driving.

net profits: the total amount of money earned after all costs are subtracted

Word Study

 University Word List Vocabulary

adapt	consume	huge
assemble	decade	luxury
automatic	economy	option
available	feature	research
component	function	version

Understanding Words

Word Parts

A useful way to figure out the meaning of a word is to look at the way it is put together. Consider the parts of the following words.

	Prefix	*Root*	*Suffix*
malfunction inappropriate researcher useless	mal- + in- +	function appropriate research + use +	-er -less

Mal- (meaning *bad* or *wrong*) and *in-* (meaning *not*) are prefixes, that is, groups of letters that have been added to the beginning of a word to give it a new meaning. *Function, appropriate, research,* and *use* are roots, that is, they carry the basic meaning of the word. *-Er* (meaning *one who . . .*) and *-less* (meaning *without*) are suffixes, letters added at the end of a word to change its meaning.

Exercise 1: Prefixes

The prefix *auto-* means *self, own, by oneself,* or *by itself.* Match each word with its definition by writing the letter of the correct definition on the line.

___ 1. autobiography
___ 2. autograph
___ 3. autonomous
___ 4. automatic
___ 5. autocrat

a. done without thinking about it
b. self-governing
c. a person's life story written by him- or herself
d. a dictator
e. the signature of a celebrity

Exercise 2: Roots

The root *dec* means *ten*. Match each word with its definition by writing the letter of the correct definition on the line.

___ 1. decade
___ 2. decathlon
___ 3. decimate
___ 4. decagon
___ 5. decapod
___ 6. deciliter
___ 7. Decalogue
___ 8. Decameron

a. a crustacean (like a crab) with ten feet
b. a ten-sided geometric figure
c. a period of ten years
d. an athletic contest consisting of ten events
e. one-tenth of a liter
f. the Ten Commandments
g. Bocaccio's literary masterpiece (divided into ten parts)
h. to kill every tenth one

Exercise 3: Suffixes

When added to words as suffixes, *-ant*, *-er*, and *-ist* often mean *one who* . . . For example, an *assistant* is someone who helps, a *teacher* is someone who teaches, and a *violinist* is someone who plays the violin. What do you call the following people?

1. someone who designs a car   a car _____

2. someone who is an expert on economics   an _____

3. someone who researches market trends   a market _____

4. someone who keeps the company accounts   an _____

5. someone who provides entertainment   an _____

Word Relationships

Another useful way to learn words is to learn them in terms of how they relate to other words in the language. Words can relate to each other in a number of ways, for example, as synonyms, antonyms, or compounds or as belonging together under the same category.

Synonyms are words that are very close in meaning to each other.
   Synonyms for *happy* are *glad, joyous, cheerful,* or *delighted.*
Antonyms are words that are opposite in meaning to each other. *Hate,*
   aversion, and *loathing* are antonyms to *love.*
Compounds are a fixed combination of two or three words that conveys a
   particular meaning *(user friendly, self-evident, baby boom).* Compounds
   can be written as one word *(baseball)* or as two words *(top*
   management, public relations). It is useful to learn a compound not as
   an individual word, but as one, fixed unit of meaning.
Categories can best be understood by looking at this information.

animals   = category
                   (also called superordinate or head word)
dog, seal, elephant = words that fit under the head word
                   (also called hyponyms)

How do *dog, seal,* and *elephant* relate to each other? They all fit under the category *animals,* that is to say, they do not equal *animals* but are included in the category *animals.*

Exercise 4: Synonyms and Antonyms

Identify the following pairs of words as synonyms (*S*) or antonyms (*A*).

___ 1. huge/enormous   ___ 5. component/part
___ 2. economical/wasteful   ___ 6. available/accessible
___ 3. optional/required   ___ 7. function/role
___ 4. feature/characteristic   ___ 8. assemble/disperse

Exercise 5: Categories

Based on your own experience and knowledge, list some words that fit under the two categories. Follow the examples.

Economy Cars   *Luxury Cars*

Falcon   Thunderbird

_____   _____

_____   _____

_____   _____

Exercise 6: Compounds

Some of the compounds in your reading appear here. Can you match them with their definitions?

___ 1. economy car
___ 2. top management
___ 3. baby boom
___ 4. showroom
___ 5. luxury car

a. the chief executives, the decision makers
b. a place where products are displayed
c. an elegant, expensive car full of options
d. a temporary increase in the birthrate
e. a car that is inexpensive to run and maintain

The Grammar of Words

Another useful strategy for learning a word is to attend to its grammar. What word family does it belong to? What part of speech is it? If a verb, is it regular or irregular? If a noun, is it countable or uncountable? If an adjective, is it generally followed by a preposition? Part of what is involved in learning a word is paying attention to the grammatical patterns in which the word occurs.

Derivatives or Word Families

Words can be learned as derivatives, as part of word families. Consider the word *economy*. Some common derivatives of the word are *economics*, *economist*, *economical*, *economically*, and *economize*. Generally, the words in the family are different parts of speech.

noun	economy, economics
noun (a person)	economist
adjective	economical
adverb	economically
verb	economize

As you are learning derivatives, remember that not all words have every part of speech in their word family.

Exercise 7: Derivatives

Complete each sentence with the word *economy* or one of its derivatives.

1. One of the main aims of the United Nations is to grant aid to

   _____ undeveloped countries.

2. Which car was more _____ to run, the Falcon or the Mustang?

3. Has the _____ of the country improved in the last decade?

4. During the oil crisis, it became necessary to _____ on gas.

5. _____ is the science that deals with the production and distribution of wealth and goods.

6. Usually, a large company hires an _____ to keep track of how its products are doing in the consumer market.

Understanding Words in Sentences

Guessing from Context

One strategy for finding out the meaning of an unknown word is to consult your dictionary. Another is to try to reason out its meaning by using context clues. There are various types of context clues.

a. *a brief definition or synonym*

> Economics is *the study of the production and distribution of goods.*
> To build the Mustang, he had no *option,* no *choice,* but to use available components.

b. *an example*

> Luxury cars *such as the Jaguar and the BMW* are status symbols.

c. *a contrast*

> There were equally interesting changes going on among older car buyers. We were now starting to see *a shift away from the economical cars* of the late 1950s that had helped the Falcon set new records. Consumers were beginning to look *beyond the plain and the purely functional* to consider *more luxurious models.*

d. *an inference*

> But the question was: could we afford the car? The answer lay in using *available components.* The *car parts for the Falcon already existed,* so if we could adapt them, we wouldn't have to start from scratch. We could build the new car with the old parts of the Falcon and save a fortune.

e. *a direct explanation*

> The notion that *decimate* means to kill every tenth person may seem strange today since, at present, the word commonly means

to kill a huge number of people. However, a long time ago the word was used to describe the common wartime practice of separating groups of captured soldiers at random and then killing every tenth one.

Exercise 8: Context Clues

Read the following passages. Then identify which of the context clues (*a.* a brief definition or synonym, *b.* an example, *c.* a contrast, *d.* an inference, *e.* a direct explanation) suggests the meaning of the underlined word or phrase.

___ 1. It was all the <u>options</u>—the automatic transmission, sidewall tires, and radios, that made the Mustang so popular.

___ 2. It made no sense to build elegant, <u>luxurious</u> cars during an oil shortage.

___ 3. Unlike the Thunderbird, which had been such a great disappointment, the Mustang was <u>flourishing</u>.

___ 4. In car manufacturing, the <u>assembly line</u> process consists of pulling the chassis or body of the car through a number of stations. At each of these stations, the car gets another part. At one, it gets the engine, at another the tires, and at still another, the seats. By the end of the line, the car is generally assembled.

___ 5. We had thought we would sell seventy-five thousand units during the first year. But the <u>projections</u> kept growing, and before the car was even out, we were planning on sales of two hundred thousand.

Exercise 9: Word Meanings in Context

In the reading passage, scan for the words and phrase given in the following list. The number of the paragraph containing the word or phrase is given in parentheses. Circle the letter of the meaning that is most appropriate within the context of the reading passage.

1. new decade (2)
   a. the fifties
   b. the 1960s
   c. 10 years

2. economy (3)
   a. expensive
   b. designed to save money
   c. sporty

3. functional (3)
  a. damaged
  b. useful
  c. extravagant

4. huge (10)
  a. little
  b. tiny
  c. enormous

5. feature (5)
  a. a movie program
  b. physical beauty
  c. characteristic

6. versions (8)
  a. translation
  b. exception
  c. slightly different forms

7. component (9)
  a. radio
  b. part
  c. ingredient

8. automatic (12)
  a. self-acting
  b. involuntary
  c. mechanical

Exercise 10: Words in Context

Complete each sentence using one of the words from the following list. Change the word form by adding -s, -ed, or -ing if necessary.

consume   huge   function
automatic   available   research

1. O'Keeffe's _____ passion for the desert is clearly evident in her landscapes.

2. Many of the facts in the report are completely false; they should have been thoroughly _____ before publication.

3. Funds were not _____ at the time for adding a new wing to the hospital.

4. Very little is known about the people who carved the _____ stone sculptures of Easter Island.

5. The _____ of language is twofold: to communicate ideas and to establish personal relationships.

6. Her reaction was purely _____ ; without thinking, she wrote a letter of resignation and walked out the door.

Using Words in Communication

For many years, vocabulary was taught as isolated items in a word list or as the components of sentences. We now realize that words are rarely used by themselves or simply to generate sentences. Rather, words are used to listen to conversations, talk to friends, read newspapers, or write letters. In the following exercises you will use words as they are used in listening, speaking, reading, or writing—as they are used in actual communication.

Exercise 11: Listening and Writing

Listen to the text on the audiotape until you understand it fairly well. With the recorder off, write down as much of the paragraph as you can remember. Then your teacher will help you compare your paragraph with the one on the tape.

Exercise 12: Dialogues

Memorize the following dialogues. Then practice the dialogues with other students.

1. *A:* May I see Mr. Williams?
   B: He's not available right now.
   A: Is he in the building?
   B: No, he's at some government function downtown.
   A: The opening of the new research institute?
   B: Yes, that's it. Mr. Williams is one of the main speakers.

2. *C:* Anything interesting in the paper today?
   D: As a matter of fact, yes. Two very good features on the economy.
   C: So, what's new with the economy?
   D: Supposedly, it's the best it's ever been.

3. *E:* Harry says you got fired yesterday.
    F: Well, that's Harry's version of the story.
    E: Oh, so you weren't fired? You quit?
    F: I quit. I just wasn't adapting very well to a ten-hour workday.

Exercise 13: Writing

Using the following outline, write a short essay about the consumer trends in the late 1950s and early 1960s that led Ford to develop the Mustang.

Consumer Trends
1. Changing economy
    a. The American economy is thriving.
    b. Consumers have more money to buy cars.
2. New kind of consumers
    a. young consumers
        (1) ready to start a family
        (2) leaving the city and moving into the suburbs
        (3) needing two cars
    b. older consumers
        (1) no longer interested in economy cars
        (2) interested in sportier and more luxurious cars
    c. single women
        (1) trained during wartime for all kinds of jobs
        (2) joining the workforce
        (3) want a car that reflects their new independence
        (4) want a car with great style and performance

Exercise 14: Reading

Compare your essay with one written by another student.

Unit 2
Maya Lin

Vocabulary Preview

Preview 1

Complete each sentence with the most suitable word.

adjustments   quote   site   appropriate   complicated

1. After agreeing to design the memorial, Lin had to go down to

   Montgomery and see the _____.

2. "The minute I read King's _____, I knew that the whole
   piece had to be about water," Lin said.

3. It occurred to her that in the warm climate of Alabama, the cooling

   effect of water would be _____.

4. Although _____ and difficult to construct, the memorial was
   dedicated on time.

5. Last-minute _____ to the structure took the workers well into
   the night.

Preview 2

Look at the way the underlined words are used in the sentences. Match
each word with its definition by writing the letter of the correct
definition on the line.

1. Phoebe, the outermost satellite of Saturn, is about 136 miles in
   diameter.
2. A bathing suit is not appropriate wear for the classroom.
3. The Supreme Court is the final court of appeal in the nation.
4. Migration, commerce, and political change continue to complicate
   language patterns in many parts of Asia.
5. Since the 1930s, scientists have known that the Sun and other stars
   generate their energy by nuclear fusion.

___ 1. diameter

___ 2. appropriate

___ 3. supreme

___ 4. complicate

___ 5. generate

a. straight line going from one side of a circle to the other side, passing through its center

b. make more difficult to understand or to use

c. produce, bring into existence

d. highest in authority, importance, or rank

e. suitable, correct, right

Reading Preview: What Do You Know about Maya Lin?

Circle the correct answer. If you don't know the answer, guess.

1. Maya Lin is a renowned
    a. Chinese American
    b. Japanese American
    c. Native American
    d. Mexican American

2. At age 21, Maya Lin won a national competition for designing
    a. a presidential library
    b. a war memorial
    c. a sculpture for a train station
    d. a mobile for a museum

3. In the United States today, "the Wall" refers to
    a. a Washington, D.C., war memorial
    b. a famous historic structure of the Civil War
    c. a ruin of the Revolutionary War
    d. a painting of a war scene

Adapted from *Maya Lin: Architect and Artist* by Mary Malone (Springfield, N.J.: Enslow Publishers, 1995), 73–81.

Introduction to the Readings

In 1981, Maya Lin became nationally known for having won a national competition to design a war memorial. The memorial, commissioned by a group of war veterans, was intended to pay tribute to members of the military who had died in the Vietnam War. Many well-known architectural and engineering firms had entered the competition. Yet the winner was a twenty-one-year-old student from Yale who had created her design as an assignment for a class in burial architecture.

Like the Vietnam War itself, Maya Lin's design turned out to be very controversial. It caused much argument and disagreement among members of the military, the government, and the general public. Instead of designing a sculpture or memorial building, Maya had designed a V-shaped wall made of polished black stone on which the names of the dead and missing were to be etched in gold. Many people were offended by "the Wall." There were newspaper attacks, hearings, and even personal attacks against Maya, in particular, insulting comments about her Chinese American background.

Today, however, "the Wall," as the Vietnam Veterans War Memorial has come to be known, is regarded as a treasured work of art. People from all over the country come to see it, to run their fingers over the names of loved ones, to leave notes, flowers, poems, and . . . to remember. The Wall is, in fact, the most visited historical site in Washington, D.C. It attracts millions of visitors every year.

The following selection, from Mary Malone's *Maya Lin: Architect and Artist*, gives an account of the design, development, and construction of a second memorial undertaken by Lin, the Civil Rights Memorial, in Montgomery, Alabama.

Reading 1: The Civil Rights Memorial—Design, Development, and Construction

(1)   After completing the Vietnam Veterans War Memorial, Maya Lin had said that she would never design another memorial. The initial controversy over her design had discouraged her. So she had retreated into her private life, doing her own kind of work and accepting some private commissions, which

she discovered she liked. "I'm interested in the psychology of the client," she said at the time.

(2)   In the spring of 1988, Maya Lin was at work in her studio when she received a call from a representative of the Southern Poverty Law Center, or SPLC, of Montgomery, Alabama. The organization had been founded in 1971 to protect and advance the legal rights of poor people and minorities. On the phone, the representative told her that the SPLC had decided to erect a civil rights memorial and wanted Maya Lin to undertake the project.

(3)   Lin did not immediately accept the commission. She said that she would read the material the SPLC wished to send her and would consider the matter. She took some time to do this, and then she accepted the commission. The historical significance of the **civil rights movement** had impressed her. She was surprised that there was no such memorial already in existence. She was also concerned that she herself knew so little about the movement, never having studied it in school. Of course, she had been a young child during the 1960s when the important marches and the landmark legal decisions had taken place. She was only eight when Martin Luther King, Jr., was assassinated. Lin said that although there were specific monuments to certain people connected with the civil rights movement, "No memorial existed that caught what the whole era was about. It had been very much a people's movement, yet many people, who had given their lives for it, had been largely forgotten."

(4)   After agreeing to design the memorial, Lin had to see the site. On the plane going to Montgomery, she reread some of the words of Dr. King. She came across—again—what he had said in several of his speeches. "We will not be satisfied until justice rolls down like waters, and righteousness like a mighty stream." "Suddenly," Lin said, "**something clicked** and the form took shape. The minute I hit that quote I knew that the whole piece had to be about water." The longer she considered it, the more certain she was. "I wanted to work with water, and I wanted to use the words of Dr. King, because that is the clearest way to remember history."

civil rights movement: A mass movement started by African Americans in the 1950s for the purpose of breaking down the established practice, in the South, of keeping blacks and whites segregated, or separated from each other. Through nonviolent means, the movement was able to gain passage of a number of significant equal-rights laws that greatly improved the lives, not just of African Americans, but of other American minorities as well. Many people lost their lives in the struggle, including the leader of the movement, Dr. Martin Luther King, Jr.
something clicked: All of a sudden, something came to mind or made sense.

(5)   She kept thinking about the form of the memorial as she continued her journey. It occurred to her that in the warm climate of Alabama, the cooling effect of flowing water would be appropriate. When she met the members of the SPLC she quickly sketched what she had in mind. Later, at the site where the memorial would stand, Lin saw the possibilities—and the need for rearranging some existing features there. It was agreed that she would start on the design as soon as she returned to New York.

(6)   The SPLC's plan in 1988 was to memorialize those individuals who had been killed in the course of marches and demonstrations for civil rights. On the memorial, their names and the names of important events in the civil rights struggle would be carved. The research of records was done by Sara Bulard, one of the directors of the SPLC and editor of the center's book about the civil rights movement, *Free at Last*. Fifty-three significant entries would be written on the memorial. When Lin saw that list, she said she realized that creating a time line was the only way to highlight those names and events. They would be listed in chronological order from the first—"May 1954, the Supreme Court ruling outlawing school segregation"—to the last, "4 April, 1968, Martin Luther King, Jr., assassinated." There would be room at both ends for additions if related names and events were discovered.

(7)   Back in her studio, Lin started work on the project. The memorial she had decided to design would be in two parts and was scheduled to be dedicated in the fall of 1989. There would be a huge granite disk, or table, twelve feet in diameter, inscribed with the fifty-three names and events. The table, with the names arranged chronologically in a circle around the perimeter, would look something like a sundial. Behind the large disk there would be a black granite wall, nine feet high, that would be inscribed with the text that had inspired Lin's design.

(8)   In the completed, functioning memorial, water flows down the wall in a gentle waterfall over those words. The table below the wall was designed to be less than three feet from the ground, made low so that children could reach it. The table, which is narrower at the bottom, from a distance appears to be floating on air. Water rising from the center of the table spreads over it, covering the time line of names and events, which is still clearly seen through the veil of water. Visitors are expected to touch the names as they walk around the table.

(9)   In the fall of 1988, not long after Lin had completed the civil rights memorial design, a fire broke out in the building where she lived and worked. Fortunately, she had, some time before, mailed the model she'd made to the

SPLC in Montgomery. Also fortunately, most of her other works were in a gallery, so her loss was minimal. But, as she explained to a journalist from the *Washington Post* who interviewed her shortly after the fire, even what she lost was not critical. She, like many other artists, often destroyed a finished sculpture or other work if for some reason she was not satisfied with it. She would start over. The important thing was that no one had been hurt in the fire.

Reading 2: The Civil Rights Memorial—The Dedication

...UNTIL JUSTICE ROLLS DOWN LIKE WATERS
AND RIGHTEOUSNESS LIKE A MIGHTY STREAM

MARTIN LUTHER KING, JR.

Civil Rights Memorial outside the Southern Poverty Law Center. Photo by Penny Weaver. Reprinted with permission.

(10)   The Civil Rights Memorial was dedicated on time, although it had been complicated and difficult to construct. Ken Upchurch, who supervised the construction, said when he first studied the specifications of the design that it was a **"contractor's nightmare."** The day before the memorial was to be unveiled, the workers as well as the anxious SPLC people wondered if the

contractor's nightmare: The contractor is the person who builds what the architect or engineer has designed. His or her "nightmare" is having to build something that is really difficult to build.

water was going to work as well as it was supposed to. Last-minute adjustments took the workers well into the night. Then, when the memorial was finally, hopefully, ready, all those present held their breath as the water was turned on. A cheer went up when the water began its slow movement down the wall and across the table. Ken Upchurch said, "It worked perfectly."

(11) Besides being visited by families, friends, and relatives of those whose names are there, the memorial attracts people from all over. Tourists come to or stop off in Montgomery to see it. As Maya Lin had hoped, the memorial has become an educational experience. Schoolchildren come and learn. Maya Lin, who had aimed for simplicity, said of the Civil Rights Memorial, "A child can understand it. You don't need to read an art book to understand it." One little girl said, "It makes you want to touch the names with your fingers and talk about what happened." Like the Vietnam Wall, where visitors weep as they touch the names of the dead and the missing, this memorial, too, evokes tears from the many people who visit it.

(12) Maya Lin was impressed, as she said, with the powerful effect that "words joined with water would generate." She was "surprised and moved when people started to cry." Tears were becoming part of the memorial, as William Zinsser wrote in *Smithsonian Magazine*.

(13) Lin received unqualified praise for her part in this memorial. Unlike the Vietnam Veterans War Memorial, this one was happily free from controversy. One writer commented, "She has once again created an architectural masterpiece." Lin herself said, "I've been incredibly fortunate to have been given the opportunity to work on not just one but both memorials."

(14) Morris Dees, founder of the SPLC, said about the memorial Lin had created for the center, "You can't put it anywhere else than in Montgomery, where everything happened, and you can't get anyone better than Maya Lin to do it."

Comprehension Check

Check your understanding of the reading selections by marking these sentences true (*T*) or false (*F*).

___ 1. At age 21, Maya Lin won a competition for designing the Vietnam Veterans War Memorial.

___ 2. Lin's design for the Vietnam Veterans War Memorial met with unqualified praise.

___ 3. The Vietnam Veterans War Memorial is a wall made of polished black stone.

___ 4. The SPLC was founded in 1971 to protect and advance the rights of veterans of the Vietnam War.

___ 5. In 1988, Maya Lin was commissioned to design a civil rights memorial.

___ 6. Lin accepted the commission immediately because she had always been impressed by what she had learned in school about the movement.

___ 7. Lin's design of the civil rights memorial was based on a quote from a speech delivered by Dr. Martin Luther King, Jr.

___ 8. Lin was impressed with the many notes and flowers people left by the Civil Rights Memorial.

Word Study

University Word List Vocabulary

adjust	generate	quote
appropriate	impression	site
complicate	legal	specify
diameter	minimum	supreme
evoke	psychology	text

Understanding Words

Word Parts

Exercise 1: Roots

The root *min*, meaning *a small size*, is the base stem for such words as *minimum, minute, miniature, minimal, minimize, minor, minority,* and *mince.* Study these sentences. Circle the letter of the item that best completes the statement or answers the question.

1. Because Mr. Lawrence was so ill, hospital visits were kept to a *minimum.* Mr. Lawrence
   a. was not allowed any visits at all
   b. had very few visits
   c. did not know who was allowed to visit

2. Before the nineteenth century, westerners' knowledge about Japanese culture was *minimal.* Before the nineteenth century, the West
   a. had incorrect information about Japan
   b. had very little information about Japan
   c. had no information at all about Japan

3. The doctor said John's burns in the fire were *minor* ones. How badly was John hurt?
   a. seriously
   b. very little
   c. not at all

4. A Chihuahua is a *miniature* dog with large pointed ears that originally came from Mexico. What most characterizes a Chihuahua is that it is very
   a. tiny
   b. wiry
   c. excitable

5. The three leading American *minorities* are African Americans, Hispanics, and Native Americans. In the United States, Hispanics are
   a. in the majority
   b. as numerous as whites
   c. a small part of the population

Word Relationships

Exercise 2: Synonyms

Cross out the word in each series that is not a synonym for the first word in that series. Use your dictionary if necessary.

1. legal	allowed	lawful	prohibited	authorized
2. adjust	adapt	fit	specify	accommodate
3. supreme	greatest	lowest	best	highest
4. appropriate	unsuitable	becoming	right	correct
5. complicated	involved	intricate	simple	complex
6. site	location	building	position	area

Exercise 3: Antonyms

Match each word on the left with its antonym by writing the letter of the correct antonym on the line. Use your dictionary if necessary.

___ 1. automatic   a. illegal
___ 2. minimum   b. simple
___ 3. appropriate   c. luxurious
___ 4. legal   d. manual
___ 5. complicated   e. maximum
___ 6. economical   f. unsuitable

Analogies

Analogies are comparisons between two sets of words. Analogies consist of four words, three of which are always given. The analogy is completed by adding a fourth word to complete the connection.

Example:

    A waiter is to a restaurant as a teller is to a bank.
        waiter : restaurant :: teller : _____

    A doctor is to the body as a dentist is to teeth.
        doctor : body :: dentist : _____

    The Bible is to Christians as the Koran is to Moslems.
        Bible : Christians :: Koran : _____

Exercise 4: Analogies

Use one of the words from the word lists in Units 1 and 2 to complete the analogy. Change the word form by adding a word ending if necessary.

1. improper : unsuitable :: suitable : _____

2. study of groups : sociology :: study of the mind : _____

3. function : functional :: option : _____

4. Falcon : economy :: Mercedes Benz : _____

5. economy : economist :: research: _____

6. car : car buyer :: goods : _____

7. adjust : adjustment :: impress : _____

8. 7 days : week :: 10 years : _____

The Grammar of Words

Exercise 5: Derivatives

Look up the derivatives of *impress* in your dictionary. Use *impress* or one of its derivatives to complete each sentence. (A derivative may be used more than once.)

1. Sandy is at a very _____ age; she's quickly influenced by everything and everyone.

2. The article aims to _____ the reader with the wisdom of saving money.

3. The exhibition was _____ ; it featured over 200 modern paintings.

4. I was under the _____ that formal wear was not required for the dinner.

5. Ellen did not make a good _____ because she was too nervous.

Phrasal Verbs

Phrasal verbs consist of a verb and a preposition (for example, *account for*) or a verb and an adverb (for example, *paid off*). Keep in mind that a phrasal verb often has a different meaning than its parts. *Paid* means *gave someone money* and *off* means *away*. *Paid off*, as in *The move paid off*, however, means *worked out well* or *was a good idea*.

Exercise 6: Phrasal Verbs

Look at how each verb is used in the reading (the number in parentheses indicates the paragraph where the verb appears), then match it with its meaning by writing the letter of the correct definition on the line.

___ 1. turn out (Introduction)   a. begin suddenly
___ 2. break out (9)   b. start the flow of
___ 3. start over (9)   c. do it again from the beginning
___ 4. turn on (10)   d. result in, prove to be, eventually

Word Meanings

Exercise 7: Word Meanings

In general, which of the items on the following list of clothing would
you consider *appropriate* wear for around the house? the beach? school?
work? a formal dance? Fill in the chart with your personal choices. If
you would never wear a particular item, leave it out.

bathing suit	tuxedo	sandals	long dress
jeans	robe	shorts	slippers
business suit	dress	boots	sweater
skirt	uniform	jumper	sweat pants

House	Beach	School	Work	Formal Dance
_____	_____	_____	_____	_____
_____	_____	_____	_____	_____
_____	_____	_____	_____	_____
_____	_____	_____	_____	_____
_____	_____	_____	_____	_____

Collocations

Collocations are words that commonly go together. Consider, for
example, common collocations with *consumer*, one of the vocabulary
words from Unit 1: *consumer credit, consumer goods, consumer spending.*

Exercise 8: Collocations

Match the adjectives with the nouns in as many combinations as
possible by writing the combinations on the lines following the
adjectives.

Example: legal aid, legal age, legal holiday

Nouns

tests	evaluation	age	issues
income	aid	holiday	rights
wage	matters	speed	

Adjectives

1. legal

_____

_____

2. psychological

_____

_____

3. minimum

_____

_____

4. adjusted

_____

_____

Understanding Words in Sentences

Exercise 9: Word Meanings in Context

Reread the following passages from the text. Then complete the sentences or answer the questions by circling the letter of the correct choice.

1. "I'm interested in the *psychology of the client*," Maya Lin said at the time.

   Maya was interested in
   a. what the client wanted to buy
   b. how much the client knew about art
   c. what the client thought about things

2. The organization had been founded in 1971 to protect and advance the *legal rights* of poor people and minorities.

   What people often need to have their legal rights defended?
   a. educated people
   b. people with little or no money
   c. wealthy people

3. The historical significance of the civil rights movement had *impressed* her. She was surprised that there was no such memorial already in existence.

   Impressed in this context means
   a. angered
   b. depressed
   c. affected

4. It occurred to Lin that in the warm climate of Alabama, the cooling effect of flowing water *would be appropriate*.

   In this case *would be appropriate* means
   a. would cost very little
   b. would fit in well
   c. would be incompatible

5. When Lin met the members of the committee she quickly sketched what she had in mind. Later, *at the site,* Lin saw the need for rearranging some existing features to fit her design.

   At the site in this case means
   a. where the memorial would stand
   b. where Lin had made her sketch
   c. where the committee had its office

6. There would be a huge granite disk, or table, twelve feet *in diameter,* inscribed with the fifty-three names and events.

How big would the table be?
a. twelve feet from the center of the table to the outside edge
b. twelve feet around the edge of the table
c. twelve feet from one side of the table to the other

Exercise 10: Collocations

This paragraph is about the civil rights movement. Underline the words or phrases associated with the movement.

Lin did not immediately accept the commission. She said that she would read the material the SPLC wished to send her and would consider the matter. She took some time to do this, and then she accepted the commission. The historical significance of the civil rights movement had impressed her. She was surprised that there was no such memorial already in existence. She was also concerned that she herself knew so little about the movement, never having studied it in school. Of course, she was a very young child during the 1960s when the marches and the landmark legal decisions had taken place. She was only eight when Martin Luther King, Jr., was assassinated. Lin said that although there were specific monuments to certain people connected with the civil rights movement, "No memorial existed that caught what the whole era was about. It had been very much a people's movement, yet many people, who had given their lives for it, had been largely forgotten."

Using Words in Communication

Exercise 11: Reading

Read about one of the works created by Maya Lin. Use the following suggestions to help you find material on this subject. Go to the library. Consult recent encyclopedia yearbooks and the library catalogs or ask the reference librarian to help you locate information. You may also want to look on the Internet by using a web-browser like "Yahoo."

Suggestions
1. Vietnam War Memorial—Washington, D.C.
2. Civil Rights Memorial—Montgomery, Alabama
3. Juniata Peace Chapel—Huntingdon, Pennsylvania
4. Women's Table—Yale University, New Haven, Connecticut
5. Eclipsed Time—Penn Station, New York City, New York

Exercise 12: Speaking

Use the following questions to interview another student about the work he or she has researched for Exercise 11.

1. What is it?
2. What is its purpose?
3. Where is it located?
4. What does it look like?
5. Who commissioned it?
6. What else do you know about it?

Then give a short three- to five-minute presentation to the class based on the interview.

Exercise 13: *Quotation* and *Quote*

The *quotations* that follow are statements said by someone else that the writer of your reading passage decided to *quote*, that is, to repeat exactly as initially uttered. As you can see, quotations generally appear inside little marks like these " " that let the reader know the writer is quoting or citing someone else. These are known as *quotation marks*.

Go back to your reading to see who is being *quoted*. Then match the quotation with the speaker.

1. "No memorial existed that caught what the whole era was about. It had been very much a people's movement—yet many people, who had given their lives for it, had been largely forgotten."

speaker: _____

2. "We will not be satisfied until justice rolls down like waters, and righteousness like a mighty stream."

speaker: _____

3. "It makes you want to touch the names with your fingers and talk about what happened."

speaker: _____

4. "You can't put it anywhere else than in Montgomery, where everything happened, and you can't get anyone better than Maya Lin to do it."

speaker: _____

Unit 3
Roberto Clemente

Vocabulary Preview

Preview 1

Complete each sentence with the most suitable word.

withdrawn   supplemented   terror   statistics   evident

1. Winner of four batting titles, Clemente was a _____ at the plate.

2. Nowhere was Clemente's love of people more _____ than in the manner of his death.

3. Today, visitors to the Hall of Fame can see a bronze tablet that lists many of the _____ that qualified Clemente for the Hall of Fame.

4. In Pittsburgh, people _____ their way of speaking with hand motions and jerks of the head.

5. During his first season, Clemente was _____, partly because he could not speak the language.

Preview 2

Look at the way the underlined words are used in the sentences. Match each word with its definition by writing the letter of the correct definition on the line.

1. Were the terrorists responsible for the bomb explosion finally brought to justice?
2. The whole time Gerald was there, Blake did not utter a single word!
3. Her emotional outburst at the wedding was quite unexpected.
4. The World Series is a postseason match between champions of the National League and the American League.
5. Maps are often used as supplements to written texts.

___ 1. terrorists   a. full of feeling
___ 2. utter   b. additions
___ 3. emotional   c. say
___ 4. series   d. violent people
___ 5. supplements   e. sequence

Reading Preview: What Do You Know about Roberto Clemente?

Circle the correct answer. If you don't know the answer, guess.

1. Roberto Clemente was born in
   a. Cuba
   b. Puerto Rico
   c. the Dominican Republic
   d. Mexico

2. Clemente was a famous
   a. baseball player
   b. basketball player
   c. tennis player
   d. golfer

3. For most of his professional career, Clemente played for
   a. the Pittsburgh Pirates
   b. the New York Yankees
   c. the Baltimore Orioles
   d. the Philadelphia Phillies

Adapted from *Who Was Roberto?* by Phil Musick (New York: Bantam Doubleday Dell, 1974), 97–105, and from *The Story of Roberto Clemente* by Jim O'Connor (New York: Bantam Doubleday Dell Books for Young Readers, 1992), 86–90, 103–4.

Introduction to the Readings

Every baseball **fan** knows Roberto Clemente, the great baseball player. Winner of four batting titles, he was a terror at the plate. In right field he acted crazy. He ran to catch pop outs behind second base, robbed batters of home runs off the walls of the baseball park, and threw out runners at all bases with one of the most powerful arms ever. He was the master player, the Great One of **Pittsburgh.**

But there was another side to Roberto Clemente. He never forgot his origins, and he worked hard to help others. He was a complex man of very powerful emotions. He had great pride in himself, in his homeland, and in his race. He was a genius on the ball field and a great human being.

Nowhere was Roberto Clemente's humanity more evident than in the manner of his death. In 1972, after batting his three thousandth hit (something that has been accomplished by only 20 other professional baseball players), Clemente returned to **Puerto Rico** for the Christmas holidays. While there, he heard about the deadly earthquake that had struck the Central American country of Nicaragua. The earthquake had destroyed the capital and had killed over seven thousand people. Clemente went into action. With the same dedication and energy he had for baseball, Clemente threw himself into the task of raising money and gathering food and clothing for the people of Nicaragua.

On New Year's Eve, Clemente boarded a plane filled with food, clothing, and medicine for the people of Nicaragua. Unfortunately, soon after taking off, the plane developed engine trouble and plunged into the Atlantic Ocean. Although a long search was conducted, no survivors were ever found. Baseball had lost one of its heroes. To honor

fan: a fanatic, someone who is very enthusiastic about something, usually a sport or a person
Pittsburgh: a city in Pennsylvania known for its steel factories and for its sports teams, here the Pittsburgh Pirates
Puerto Rico: An island in the Caribbean politically bound to the United States as a "free associated state." Puerto Ricans are American citizens.

him, the Baseball Writers Association of America voted him into baseball's Hall of Fame. He was the first **Hispanic** to be honored in this way.

The following readings provide a glimpse into two periods of Clemente's life. The first, adapted from Phil Musick's *Who Was Roberto?* gives us a look at Roberto's difficult early years in the major leagues in America. The second, adapted from Jim O'Connor's *The Story of Roberto Clemente* shows us Clemente when he was already being recognized as a true baseball champion.

Hispanic: a person whose origins can be traced back to Spanish culture and the Spanish language; an American minority including Puerto Ricans

Reading 1: A Rookie's Frustration

(1)   In the 1950s Roberto Clemente arrived in Pittsburgh to play baseball for the Pittsburgh Pirates. He was very young, just emerging from boyhood into manhood. Many things surprised Clemente about Pittsburgh. Above all, he was puzzled by people with a strange language and a strange way of speaking. They spoke English instead of Spanish, and they supplemented their way of speaking with a lot of hand gestures and jerks of the head.

(2)   Pittsburgh was as different from Puerto Rico as Paris from Peking. Where could a homesick twenty-year-old youth buy fried bananas? Or listen to the music of the *coqui,* a tiny frog that sings more sweetly than any songbird? Or hear a comforting ***Como esta usted?*** And why did black people cluster in a place called the Hill? And why did strangers laugh when you tried to speak their language? And why didn't the sun ever shine? And what was a ***nigger?***

(3)   "I couldn't speak English," Clemente said. "Not to speak the language . . . this is a terrible problem. Not to speak the language meant you were different." To be black meant you were different. Not to know that bananas were sliced on cereal instead of fried meant you were different. Being different was not easy. "Some people act as though they think I lived in a jungle," Clemente said. He was surprised years later when a woman asked if he wore a **loincloth** in Puerto Rico.

(4)   Clemente found very few friends in the Pirate clubhouse. He could be seen by himself signing autographs for fans, hours after home games. "I was lonely . . . I had nothing else to do," he said. He was also unhappy about the cool weather, and, for the first time, he was faced with an unexpected enemy: prejudice.

(5)   "I know Roberto was hurt deeply by some of the unkind comments he heard during his first years here," said one of his teammates. "He was withdrawn partly because of the language. He'd only ever been out of Puerto Rico one other time. Everything was new and confusing to him."

(6)   Nothing confused Clemente more than newspaper reporters. They often quoted his ungrammatical utterances: "I no play so gut yet . . . Me like hot weather . . . I no run fast cold weather." Why would reporters want to make fun of his English when he was trying so hard to learn it? Roberto wondered.

Como esta usted? Spanish for "How are you?"
nigger: a very insulting offensive slang word for "black person"
loincloth: A small piece of material worn wrapped around the hips. The use of a loincloth is often associated with primitive people.

Reading 2: A True Superstar

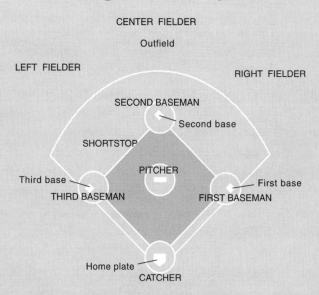

(7)   On July 24, 1970, over forty-three thousand fans packed into Three Rivers Stadium, the new home of the Pittsburgh Pirates. They came to celebrate a very special event: Roberto Clemente Night.

(8)   In June, the Pirates had played their last game at Forbes Field. Walking off the field for the last time had been tough for Roberto. He had played in Forbes Field for fifteen seasons. It had been like a second home to him. Now there was a new stadium, a new home for the team, and Roberto was being honored for his remarkable contribution to the Pirates' high standing in major league baseball.

(9)   The crowd roared when Roberto walked onto the field at Three Rivers Stadium that July evening. As he looked around Roberto saw many familiar faces. He also saw hundreds of Puerto Ricans wearing *pavas,* the brimmed straw hats that the workers wore in the sugarcane fields. Many of them had come from Puerto Rico to Pittsburgh just to attend the game. Everyone was there for the same reason—to honor Clemente.

(10)   To begin Roberto Clemente Night, all the Latin players in the Pirates lined up in front of Roberto. One by one they approached him, placed a hand on his shoulder, and gave him the *abrazo,* a ceremonial embrace. Roberto was very touched by this gesture. Then all the awards and gifts were presented to Roberto. Among other things, he was given a scroll signed by over three hundred thousand people in Puerto Rico. Roberto was also told that thou-

sands of dollars had been collected and given in his name to his favorite charity, the Pittsburgh Children's Hospital.

(11)   After the ceremony, Roberto ran out to right field. He had played with the Pirates for fifteen seasons, which had included a World Series and nine All-Star Games. He had been awarded the Most Valuable Player title, four batting titles, and ten consecutive **Gold Gloves.**

(12)   After the game Roberto told the press what had been going through his mind during the ceremony. "In a moment like this, you can see a lot of years in a few minutes . . . I don't know if I cried, but I am not ashamed to cry. We are a sentimental people. I don't have the words to say how I feel when I step out onto that field and know that so many are behind me and know that I represent my island and all of Latin America."

(13)   Today visitors to the Hall of Fame can see the bronze tablet that lists many of the statistics that qualified Clemente for the Hall of Fame. But there is a lot about Roberto that is not on the plaque. The plaque does not say that Roberto Clemente played right field with a combination of grace and power that has never been equaled. It does not say that his batting grew more powerful every year or that Roberto still inspires young ballplayers everywhere. The plaque does not say that Roberto lost his life helping people he hardly knew. It does not say that Roberto showed the people of his country, his friends, and his fans how to be proud to be black or Puerto Rican. The plaque gives the reasons why Roberto Clemente is in the Hall of Fame. But it does not mention many of the other reasons why Clemente still lives in the hearts of many, especially in the hearts of his countrymen.

Comprehension Check

Check your understanding of the reading selections by marking these sentences as true (*T*) or false (*F*).

___ 1. The Pirates are a baseball club based in Pittsburgh, Pennsylvania.

___ 2. When Clemente first started to play for the Pirates he was very homesick for his homeland, Nicaragua.

___ 3. Clemente was the Pirates' right outfielder.

Gold Gloves: an award given in baseball to players who are outstanding at catching and fielding the baseball

___ 4. Nominations for the Hall of Fame are made by baseball writers.

___ 5. Clemente is the first Hispanic to be inducted into baseball's Hall of Fame.

___ 6. Roberto Clemente Night was held in Forbes Field, the baseball park where Clemente had played ball for fifteen years.

___ 7. Clemente tried to help the victims of an earthquake in Nicaragua by collecting food, clothing, and medicine for them.

___ 8. Clemente died when terrorists bombed the airplane he was flying to Nicaragua.

Word Study

 University Word List Vocabulary

accomplish	emerge	statistic
approach	emotion	supplement
complex	evident	terror
conduct	hero	utter
embrace	series	withdraw

Understanding Words

Word Parts

Exercise 1: Roots

The root *leg*, originating in the Latin *legalis* meaning *law*, is the stem for the following words.

legal   illegal   legislate   legislature   legislator   illegitimate

Fill in each blank with one of these words to complete the definitions.

1. The _____ is the group of people in a country with the power to make and pass laws.

2. An _____ act is one that is not allowed by the laws of the country.

3. The person who makes and passes laws is called a _____.

4. _____ business activities are those that are not permitted by law.

5. The office of _____ aid will help people who do not have the money to pay for a lawyer.

6. To _____ is to pass a new law.

Exercise 2: Prefixes

Which of the following words can take the prefix *in-*? Which ones can take the prefix *un-*? Which ones can take the prefix *mis-*? Add word endings if necessary. Write the newly formed words on the lines under the correct prefixes.

appropriate	attain	complicate	quote
emotion	avail	conduct	voluntary

in-   *mis-*   *un-*

_____   _____   _____

_____   _____   _____

_____   _____   _____

_____   _____   _____

Use one of the newly formed words to complete each of the following sentences. Add word endings if necessary.

1. Dr. Sanders is going on vacation, so he will be _____ for the rest of the week.

2. Sergeant Lewis was released from his duties on charges of military

   _____.

3. The topic was very _____ to the occasion—how can you be talking about funerals at a wedding?

4. I like the _____ country life—one day is the same as another and there aren't a lot of stresses every day.

5. You are _____ Laertes. It wasn't he who said, "Get thee to a nunnery." It was Hamlet.

6. Everyone was surprised that Miriam cried so much at her father's remarriage. She's generally so _____!

Word Relationships

Exercise 3: Synonyms

Cross out the word in each series that is not a synonym for the first word in that series. Use your dictionary if necessary.

1. accomplish   achieve   attain   complete   abandon
2. hero   champion   victor   loser   conqueror
3. conduct   behavior   guide   manners   demeanor
4. utter   hear   speak   say   talk
5. terror   fear   alarm   panic   concern
6. emotion   indifference feeling   sympathy   sentiment

The Grammar of Words

Exercise 4: Derivatives

Look up the derivatives of *terror* in a dictionary. Use *terror* or one of its derivatives to complete each sentence.

1. One of the largest acts of _____ in the United States was the bombing of a federal building in Oklahoma.

2. Are the _____ who planted a bomb in the World Trade Center in jail?

3. Since childhood, he has been _____ of lightning.

4. The explosion of the Challenger was a _____ spectacle.

5. The older boys _____ the younger children with stories about ghosts and monsters.

Transitive and Intransitive Verbs

Transitive verbs are verbs that take a direct object. *Withdraw,* meaning *to pull something back, to move,* or *to remove,* is a transitive verb; it takes an object. For example:

The cat *withdrew* its *claws.*
I plan to *withdraw* my *name* from the list of candidates.
He *withdrew money* from the bank.

After we argued, I *withdrew* my *friendship*.

Withdraw, meaning *to retreat, to retire,* or *to go away from a place* is intransitive; it does not take an object. When used intransitively, the verb is often accompanied by a preposition, usually either *to* or *from*. For example:

Mrs. Holmes *withdrew from* the room.
Laura *withdrew to* the study.
Mr. Allen *withdrew from* the race.

Exercise 5: Transitive and Intransitive

Write *C* when *withdraw* is used in the sentence correctly and *I* when it is used incorrectly.

___ 1. David was thinking of withdrawing his support from the party.
___ 2. John withdrew his office to take the phone call in private.
___ 3. I want to withdraw the discussion because I don't have all the facts.
___ 4. Yesterday, I withdrew some money from the bank machine.
___ 5. He withdrew his sailboat from the race.
___ 6. After dinner, Jennifer withdraw the bed because she was very tired.

Word Meanings

Most words have more than one meaning. Consider these three meanings of the word *complex*.

A. *complex* \\'käm-ˌpleks\\ adj: consisting of two or more interrelated parts
B. *complex* \\käm-'pleks\\ adj: involved, complicated, difficult to understand
C. *complex* \\'käm-ˌpleks\\ n: a group of buildings or units related in some way

The only way to determine which meaning of *complex* applies is to look at the entire context in which it appears.

Exercise 6: Word Meanings

Use either *a, b,* or *c* to mark which meaning applies in each sentence.

— 1. Environmental pollution is a complex problem.
— 2. The new cinema complex makes it possible for customers to choose from among eight different movies.
— 3. The map indicates that there is a huge military complex in the area.
— 4. Some flower structures are very simple; others are highly complex.
— 5. Jackson is known for her excellent portrayal of complex women.
— 6. The Caucasus is a complex area of mountain ranges, plains, rivers, lakes, grasslands, and forests.

Exercise 7: Word Meanings

In psychology, *complex* is used to talk about a group of repressed desires or memories that still has a powerful influence on someone's behavior or personality. Here are some other types of complexes that you might find in your reading. Write a definition of each. Use your dictionary if necessary.

1. a superiority complex _____

2. an inferiority complex _____

3. a persecution complex _____

4. a guilt complex _____

Word Origins

Etymology is the study of the origin of a word or phrase. Consider the term *Oedipus complex*. How did it originate?

Exercise 8

Look up *Oedipus* in your dictionary.

1. Write one or two sentences identifying Oedipus. Who was he? What did he do?

   _____

   _____

2. Write one or two sentences that summarize the meaning of *Oedipus complex*.

   The term *Oedipus complex* means _____

   _____

Exercise 9: Etymology

The etymology of *psyche* in words such as *psyche, psychic, psychology, psychiatry,* and *psychoanalysis* can be traced all the way back to Psyche, a princess in Greek and Roman mythology who was the personification of the human soul and mind. Knowing the etymology of *psyche,* can you match the words on the left with their definitions?

___ 1. psyche
___ 2. psychic
___ 3. psychiatrist
___ 4. psychology
___ 5. psychoanalysis

a. a doctor who treats mental illness
b. the human soul or mind
c. a method developed by Sigmund Freud to treat mental disorders
d. the study of the mind and mental processes
e. a person who, supposedly, connects with spirits outside the physical world

Understanding Words in Sentences

Exercise 10: Word Meanings in Context

Reread the following passages from the text. Then complete the
sentences or answer the questions by circling the letter of the correct
choice.

1. In the 1950s Roberto Clemente arrived in Pittsburgh to play baseball
   for the Pittsburgh Pirates. He was very young, just emerging from
   boyhood into manhood.

   Emerging in this case means
   a. coming out of
   b. becoming visible
   c. disappearing

2. Many things surprised Clemente about Pittsburgh. Above all, he was
   puzzled by people with a strange language and a strange way of
   speaking. They spoke English instead of Spanish, and they
   supplemented their way of speaking with a lot of hand gestures and
   jerks of the head.

   Supplemented their way of speaking means the people of Pittsburgh
   a. used their hands and heads a lot when they spoke
   b. were very stiff and rigid
   c. became very emotional

3. After the ceremony, Roberto ran out to right field. He had played
   with the Pirates for fifteen seasons, which had included a World
   Series and nine All-Star Games. He had been awarded the Most
   Valuable Player title, four batting titles, and ten consecutive Gold
   Gloves.

   This paragraph is about
   a. Clemente's feelings about baseball
   b. Clemente's reaction to being honored by the Pirates
   c. Clemente's accomplishments

4. Today visitors to the Hall of Fame can see the bronze tablet that lists many of the statistics that qualified Clemente for the Hall of Fame. But there is a lot about Roberto that is not on the plaque. The plaque does not say that Roberto Clemente played right field with a combination of grace and power that has never been equaled. It does not say that his batting grew more powerful every year or that Roberto still inspires young ballplayers everywhere. The plaque does not say that Roberto lost his life helping people he hardly knew. It does not say that Roberto showed the people of his country, his friends, and his fans how to be proud to be black or Puerto Rican. The plaque gives the reasons why Roberto Clemente is in the Hall of Fame. But it does not mention many of the other reasons why Clemente still lives in the hearts of many, especially in the hearts of his countrymen.

Choose a title for this paragraph.
a. What the Plaque Does Not Tell Us about Clemente
b. The Statistics That Entitled Clemente To Be in the Hall of Fame
c. How Clemente Died

Exercise 11: Guessing from Context

1. Can you find the meanings of the following Spanish words in the readings? Write down the meanings.

   a. coqui _____

   b. abrazo _____

   c. pava _____

2. How were you able to figure out the meanings of these words?

   _____

3. What is one good clue, then, for determining the meaning of a word in a particular context?

   Context clue: _____

Exercise 12: Collocations

These are some common collocations for words in this unit.

disorderly conduct	vital statistics
self-evident	emotional outburst
heroic act	supplementary materials

Answer the following questions based on these collocations by circling the letter of the correct answer.

1. When someone is arrested for disorderly conduct, what might he or she have been arrested for?
   a. killing someone
   b. holding someone up for money
   c. singing loudly in the street at three o'clock in the morning

2. Which of the following can one get at the Bureau of Vital Statistics?
   a. a birth certificate
   b. a driver's license
   c. a voter registration card

3. If a truth is self-evident, how complex is it?
   a. It is so complex that it needs to be explained further.
   b. It is so apparent that it does not need to be explained further.
   c. It can only be understood by a few people.

4. If a friend is very emotional at a funeral, which of the following might she be doing?
   a. putting flowers on the grave
   b. crying uncontrollably
   c. praying quietly

5. Which of the following would be considered a heroic act?
   a. entering a burning house to rescue a friend
   b. helping a friend with his vocabulary homework
   c. giving blood for a friend's operation

6. If a person buys supplementary materials for a textbook, what might he or she buy?
   a. a glossary
   b. a table of contents
   c. cassette tapes

Exercise 13: Collocations

Work with another student to make a list of words or phrases that you associate with a plane crashing into the ocean. Then compare your list with the words that are underlined in Exercise 13 in the Answer Key. Which of the words on your list are underlined in the paragraph? Which are not?

Using Words in Communication

Exercise 14: Speaking

Study the statistics of Clemente's performance in two World Series.

Year	Club	AB	H	2B	3B	HR	RBI	BA
1960	Pittsburgh Pirates	29	9	0	0	0	3	.310
1971	Pittsburgh Pirates	29	12	2	1	2	4	.414

AB = times at bat   H = single base hits   2B = two base hits
3B = three base hits   HR = home runs   RBI = runs batted in
BA = batting average; the number of hits divided by the number of times at bat

Work with another student. Ask and answer the following questions.

1. When did Clemente play in the World Series?
2. What ball club did he play for?
3. How many times was he at bat (AB) in 1960? In 1971?
4. Compare the number of home runs (HR) he batted in 1960 with the number he batted in 1971.
5. Compare his batting average (BA) in 1960 with the one in 1971.

Exercise 15: Associations

Work with two or three other students to make a list of the emotions Clemente probably experienced when

a. he first played baseball for the Pirates;
b. he heard about the earthquake in Nicaragua;
c. he was honored at Three Rivers Stadium during Roberto Clemente Night.

Write a short paragraph describing Clemente's emotional state on one of these occasions.

_____

_____

_____

_____

_____

_____

Exercise 16: Dialogues

Memorize the dialogues. Then practice them with another student.

1. *A:* When was Clemente approached by a major league team?
   B: When he was still in high school.
   A: Was he good?
   B: Are you kidding? He was outstanding! He was their all-time hero!

2. *C:* How did Clemente help the people of Nicaragua?
   D: Well, he conducted a huge drive to get them food and clothing and everything.
   C: Was it successful?
   D: Well, the drive was very successful, but he died in a plane crash when he was flying the stuff over there.

3. *E:* How was the celebration last night?

   F: It was great. A lot of the players walked up and embraced him, and everyone cheered, and he got all these gifts . . .

   E: Did he say much?

   F: Not much. He just said it was all too emotional for him.

Review Unit 1

I. Choose the correct word from the list on the left to go with each meaning. (In each set, you will not use two of the words.)

Example:

1. appropriate	<u>1</u> right
2. legal	<u>5</u> investigator
3. available	<u>2</u> allowed
4. automatic	
5. researcher	

Set A

1. embrace	—— adjust
2. approach	—— hug
3. impress	—— detail
4. adapt	
5. specify	

Set B

1. option	—— translation
2. version	—— words
3. conduct	—— behavior
4. luxury	
5. text	

Set C

1. feature	—— sentence
2. function	—— characteristic
3. series	—— feeling
4. utterance	
5. emotion	

II. Identify the following pairs of words as synonyms (*S*) or antonyms (*A*).

___ 1. series/sequence   ___ 5. text/document
___ 2. appropriate/improper   ___ 6. withdraw/take back
___ 3. option/choice   ___ 7. complicate/simplify
___ 4. site/location   ___ 8. version/account

III. Match each word on the left with a common collocation by writing the letter of the correct choice on the line.

___ 1. market   a. size
___ 2. inferiority   b. wage
___ 3. minimum   c. supplement
___ 4. assembly   d. research
___ 5. specify   e. complex
___ 6. Sunday   f. line
___ 7. self   g. conduct
___ 8. disorderly   h. evident
                     i. characteristic
                     j. document

IV. Identify each group of letters as a prefix (*P*), root (*R*), or suffix (*S*). There may be two answers for some items.

___ 1. in   ___ 6. un
___ 2. mal   ___ 7. hero
___ 3. utter   ___ 8. re
___ 4. ist   ___ 9. site
___ 5. er   ___ 10. able

V. List five context clues that you can use to figure out the meaning of a word.

1. _____

2. _____

3. _____

4. _____

5. _____

VI. Match each phrasal verb on the left with its meaning by writing the letter of the correct definition on the line.

    — 1. pay off   a. leave

    — 2. turn down   b. happen

    — 3. take place   c. start

    — 4. break out   d. give good results

    — 5. take off   e. say no

VII. Complete each sentence with one of the words given here. You may need to change the form of the word or add word endings.

utter	complex	approach	assemble
hero	conduct	adjust	feature

1. One of the nice _____ of the new model is the CD player.

2. The training session will be _____ by our supervisor.

3. The police officer thought that the man was armed, so he

    _____ him carefully.

4. The last words she _____ as she hurried toward the airplane were, "I'll e-mail you."

5. The issue is not a simple one; in some ways it is very

    _____.

6. The seat belt is too long; it needs to be _____.

7. The students _____ in the auditorium for a lecture.

8. He got a medal for his _____ actions that saved the child.

Unit 4
Maya Angelou

Vocabulary Preview

Preview 1

Complete each sentence with the most suitable word.

residing   comprehend   cultures   assigned   layer

1. I opened the package carefully and pulled the last _____ of paper away.

2. If we didn't want our rooms to be _____ arbitrarily, we had to choose our own roommates and let him know.

3. His words ran together, and it was difficult for me to _____ them.

4. In many _____ there is the belief that all things have spirits living in them.

5. When a drummer prepares to make a new drum, he approaches the tree he will use and prays to the spirit _____ there.

Preview 2

Look at the way the underlined words are used in the sentences. Match each word with its definition by writing the letter of the correct definition on the line.

1. Saul Bass was a graphic designer who created advertising symbols for many companies and won an Academy Award for his film *Why Man Creates*.

2. It is easy to conceive of possessing things that can be touched, but it is difficult to conceive of possessing a right, a privilege, or a power.

3. There was a Jewish revolt while Nero was emperor of Rome.

4. The concept of holy war is found in the Christian Bible and has also played a role in many other religions.

5. Shakespeare wrote some of the best-known <u>dramas</u> of Elizabethan theater.

___ 1. create   a. rebellion, uprising
___ 2. conceive   b. to make
___ 3. revolt   c. a serious play
___ 4. concept   d. to imagine, to understand
___ 5. drama   e. idea

Reading Preview: What Do You Know about Maya Angelou?

Circle the correct answer. If you don't know the answer, guess.

1. Maya Angelou is
   a. a famous movie star
   b. an architect
   c. a writer, poet, and playwright
   d. a U.S. congresswoman

2. As a young woman Maya
   a. attended an all-black college
   b. designed a famous monument
   c. worked as a singer and dancer
   d. became active in politics after meeting President Kennedy

3. Maya Angelou
   a. died in 1993
   b. wrote a poem for President Clinton's inauguration in 1993
   c. received the Nobel Peace Prize in 1993
   d. became the U.S. ambassador to South Africa in 1993

Adapted from *Singin' and Swingin' and Gettin' Merry Like Christmas* by Maya Angelou (New York: Random House., 1976), 132–34 and 171–76, and *Wouldn't Take Nothin' for My Journey Now* by Maya Angelou (New York: Random House, 1993), 33–35.

Introduction to the Readings

Maya Angelou was born in 1928 in a rural town in Arkansas. Today she is perhaps America's best-known contemporary black writer and poet. She wrote and read her own poem "On the Pulse of Morning" at President Clinton's inaugural address in 1993. Maya has also achieved professional success as a lecturer, a historian, an actress, a playwright, a civil rights activist, a film producer, and a director—in spite of the fact that few black women have been able to work and succeed in these areas.

Maya's writing eloquently describes her life as a black woman in a mostly white America. In the first two readings, from *Singin' and Swingin' and Gettin' Merry Like Christmas*, Maya shares some of her experiences as a young professional dancer in a production of George Gershwin's opera *Porgy and Bess*. In the last reading, from *Wouldn't Take Nothin' for My Journey Now*, Maya discusses the importance of "Spirit" and God in her life.

Reading 1: *Porgy and Bess*

(1)   I had heard the stage manager's announcement earlier, but none of the women responded. Now Martha turned away from the mirror and began to sing, "Do re me fa so la ti do." I didn't know whether I was expected to say something or not. Then Lillian also stretched her lips in a tight smile and holding her teeth closed sang, "Ye, ya, yo, you." Barbara Ann stood and began to move slowly from side to side. She started to raise and lower her jaw and then sang, "Wooo woooooo."

(2)   They took no notice of me, but I couldn't do the same with them. I had never been so close to trained singers, and the vibrations shook in my ears. I left the room and walked down the hall to find my place in the **wings.** Sounds came out of each door I passed. Grunts overlapped the high-pitched "ha ha ho hos," and the noise was so funny I could have laughed. These beautiful singers who would soon stand on the stage delivering the most lovely sounds first made noises like animals. But then I remembered that before I could dance, I had to prepare. I had to bend up and down, stretching, contracting,

wings: the sides of a theater stage behind the curtains

and releasing my muscles until they ached and I wanted to stop. The singers were not funny. They were working. Preparation is rarely easy and never beautiful. That was the first of many lessons *Porgy and Bess* taught me.

(3)   I sat on a chair in the wings and watched the singers respond to the stage manager's shouted "Places, please. Places." The singers moved directly to their places on the stage. There were a few whispers as the lights faded to black. There was applause from in front of the curtain, and the lively opening music of **George Gershwin's** opera swelled onto the stage. The curtain began sliding open, and softly colored lights lit up the set. In a rush the show began.

(4)   The singers acted as if they were indeed the poor Southern blacks whose lives rotated around the work camp of **Catfish Row.** They sang and listened. Then they harmonized with each others' voices so closely that the stage became a wall of music.

(5)   Their performance affected the audience and me. When the first act was over, the audience applauded long and loudly, and I was exhausted and covered in sweat. The singers, on the other hand, seemed to step out of their roles easily. They passed me on their way to the dressing rooms talking to each other. I disliked their lighthearted attitude. It seemed as if they had forgotten the great emotions they had sung about and aroused in me. It wasn't pleasant to discover they were only playing parts. I wanted them to walk off the stage wrapped in drama or tragedy.

Reading 2: Mr. Julian's Heart

(6)   The Moskva Hotel in **Belgrade, Yugoslavia,** was a large hotel, but it could hardly hold all of our singers, administration, and conductors. Our manager, Bob Dustin, cheerfully announced that we would have to sleep three to a room. He said that, if we didn't want our rooms assigned arbitrarily, we should choose our own roommates and let him know.

(7)   Martha, Ethel, and I agreed to share one of the large rooms. Ethel had made friends with Martha and could tolerate Martha's always sharp, often

George Gershwin: A popular American composer of the 1930s, '40s and '50s. He wrote the opera *Porgy and Bess.*
Catfish Row: the name of the poor, black town where the story of *Porgy and Bess* takes place
Belgrade, Yugoslavia: the old capital city of Yugoslavia (the area that is Serbia and Montenegro, as of 1998)

acid comments. Ethel would smile calmly and say, "Martha Flowers, you are terrible. Charming, talented, but terrible." Martha would laugh and forget her bad mood. We had expected three single beds in our room. Instead we found one large, lumpy bed, a very worn rug, and a single light. Ethel slept in the middle, and Martha slept beside the night table. She jumped when the telephone rang late one night.

(8)   "Who on earth? What time is it?" The telephone and Martha's angry voice woke up Ethel and me. Martha softened her voice. "Good morning." She sang the greeting. "Miss who?" We were all sitting upright in bed. "Miss Maya Angelou?" Her voice revealed her surprise. "And you are Mr. Julian? Hold on."

"Hello?"
"Is this Miss Maya Angelou?" The question was asked by a voice I had never heard.
"Yes, I am Maya Angelou."
"Miss Maya, I am being Mr. Julian. It's that last night I am seeing you dance. I am watching you dance across the stage and looking at your legs jumping through the air, and, Miss Maya, I am loving you."

acid comments: comments that are sarcastic or unkind; comments that burn or hurt the way acid does

His words ran together, and it was difficult for me to comprehend them. "I beg your pardon?"

"It's I am loving you, Miss Maya. It's that if you are hearing a man is throwing his body into the **Danube River** today, and dying in the icy water, that man is being me."

"Just a minute. Excuse me, what is your name?"

"I am being Mr. Julian, and I am loving you."

"Yes, well, Mr. Julian, why do you want to kill yourself? Why would loving me make you want to die? I don't think that's very nice."

Ethel and Martha were both watching me.

"Look, mister."

"It's being Mr. Julian."

"Yes, well, Mr. Julian, thanks for the telephone call—"

"May I please be seeing you? May I please be taking you to one expensive café and watching your lovely lips drink coffee with cream?"

"No, thank you. I am sorry, but I have to hang up now."

"Miss Maya, if you're not seeing me, then today I am sending you my heart."

(9)   Oh my God. The woman who gave me **Serbo-Croatian** lessons in Paris had told me solemnly that these people were passionate. They were so romantic that they would gladly injure themselves to show their love. And here this unknown man was threatening to send me his heart.

"Oh, no, Mr. Julian. Please. I beg you. Don't send me your heart."

"Miss Maya. It is that I am sending it to your theater, by hand, this morning. Good-bye, lovely legs dancing."

The line went dead.

(10)   I waited all day. Drinking wine and trying to write happy letters to my family. Finally all of the **cast members** assembled in the hotel lobby, got onto the buses, and were driven to the theater.

Danube River: the large river that runs through the city of Belgrade
Serbo-Croatian: one of the national languages of Yugoslavia; a person from Serbo-Croatia
cast members: all of the actors, actresses, dancers, and singers who perform on stage in a show

(11) "Maya, there's something in the dressing room for you." He did it. The poor man. He actually cut out his heart and had it sent to me. I kept my face calm, but my body trembled and my stomach was in revolt. I opened the dressing room door, ready to see a blood covered organ still beating like something in a horror film. A flat package wrapped in colorful paper lay on my dressing table. If it was a heart it had been cut into very thin pieces. I closed the door and picked up the box.

(12) The note read: "Miss Maya, here is my heart. I am loving you. I am wishing to see you. Good-bye, my lovely legs. Mr. Julian." He had to be alive. Otherwise how could he hope to see me? I opened the package carefully and pulled the last layer of paper away.

(13) Mr. Julian's heart was a cake.

Reading 3: In the Spirit

(14) Spirit is an invisible force made visible in all life. In many African cultures there is the belief that all things have spirits living in them. These spirits are things that must be calmed and to which a person can appeal. So, for example, when a drummer prepares to make a new drum, he approaches the tree he will use and prays to the spirit residing there. In his prayer he talks about what he plans to do. He assures the spirit that he will remain grateful

for the gift of the tree, and he promises he will use the drum only for honorable purposes.

(15)   I believe that Spirit is one and is everywhere. Spirit never leaves me. Sometimes I may withdraw from it, but I can realize its presence as soon as I return to my senses. I cannot separate what I conceive of as Spirit from my concept of God. I believe that God is Spirit.

(16)   Because I know that I am a creation of God I must realize and remember that everyone else and everything else are also God's creation. This is difficult for me when I think of cruel, violent, or prejudiced people. I would like to think that these people were not created by my God. But since I believe that God created all things, I know that these people are also children of God. And I must try to treat them as children of God.

(17)   My faith in God is tested many times every day. I begin to doubt God's love if a promise is broken, or a secret is not kept, or if I experience pain. I do not believe, and I cry out in sadness. Then the Spirit lifts me up again, and I have faith. I don't know how this happens, but when I call out to God earnestly I am answered immediately and I am returned to faith. I am once again filled with Spirit and firmly planted on solid ground.

Comprehension Check

Check your understanding of the reading selections by marking these sentences true (*T*) or false (*F*).

—   1. The singers made funny noises to warm up their voices before they went on stage.
—   2. When Maya prepared to dance she did exercises that were fun and easy.
—   3. *Porgy and Bess* is a play about a wealthy black family living in New York City.
—   4. Bob Dustin told Martha, Ethel, and Maya that they had to share a room.
—   5. Martha Flowers was a very kind, sweet woman.
—   6. Mr. Julian fell in love with Maya after he saw her perform on stage.
—   7. According to the reading selection, Serbo-Croatian people are famous for being very passionate and emotional.
—   8. Mr. Julian killed himself.
—   9. In some cultures people believe that spirits live inside all things.
—   10. Maya Angelou is an *atheist*: a person who does not believe in God.

Word Study

 University Word List Vocabulary

arbitrary	contract	muscle
assign	create	overlap
comprehend	culture	reside
conceive	drama	revolt
concept	layer	rotate

Understanding Words

Word Parts

Exercise 1: Prefixes

The prefix *mis-* means *done badly or wrongly*. Look at the way the underlined words are used in the sentences. Then match each word with its definition by writing the letter of the correct definition on the line.

1. Several students missed the third question on the test because they misspelled the answer.
2. The budget was misconceived; the company actually lost money in the first year.
3. The lawyer was fired for misconduct after accepting money from an organized crime group.
4. Economic mismanagement has recently forced several large banks out of business.
5. There were not enough seats for everyone; the number of seats needed had been miscalculated.

___ 1. misspell   a. an illegal or improper act
___ 2. misconceive   b. to organize or deal with something badly
___ 3. misconduct   c. to spell a word incorrectly
___ 4. mismanage   d. to make a mistake when judging a situation
___ 5. miscalculate   e. to not think an idea out properly

Exercise 2: Suffixes

The suffix -or is added to some verbs to form nouns. These nouns refer to a person who does a certain kind of work or who performs a certain action.

  Add the suffix -or to each of the words given here and write the new words on the lines provided. Then fill in the blanks in the following sentences with the appropriate new words.

administrate   create   demonstrate   conduct

_____   _____   _____   _____

1. I'm not sure what time the train will arrive in Boston. Let me go ask

   the _____.

2. In the classic story *Frankenstein,* Dr. Frankenstein is the _____
   of a strange manlike creature.

3. Janet works as an _____ at the City Hospital. She manages
   the patient records section.

4. _____ marched in the streets to protest the government's
   decision to raise taxes.

Can you think of any other words that use -or in this way? Write them here.

_____   _____   _____

Word Relationships

Exercise 3: Compounds

The word *contract* can be used to form many compounds. Fill in the blanks in the following sentences with one of the phrases given here.

business contract   employment contract
rental contract   marriage contract

1. All new workers must read the company handbook and agree to
   follow company policies before signing an _____.
2. The bride's family and the groom's family had agreed on the terms of
   the _____ months before the wedding day.
3. Before moving into a new apartment you are required to sign a
   _____ and pay a $500 security deposit.
4. After the meeting, representatives and lawyers from both companies
   signed the _____ that would finalize the agreement.

What is the common idea in all of the uses of *contract* in the preceding
sentences? Circle the best answer.

a. payment
b. a person who gets paid to do something
c. a legal agreement to do something

Exercise 4: Related Words

Cross out the word in each series that does not belong.

1. assign	appoint	take	name
2. concept	activity	idea	thought
3. culture	customs	opinion	traditions
4. drama	tragedy	orchestra	comedy
5. muscle	sense	bone	organ
6. overlap	cover	extend	omit
7. resident	home	dwelling	housing
8. rotate	revolve	spin	alternate
9. conceive	imagine	understand	hope
10. grasp	idea	understand	comprehend

Word Meanings

Read the three common definitions for the word *contract* given here. You will use these definitions in Exercise 5.

A. *contract* \'kän-ˌtrakt\ n: 1. an agreement between two or more persons; 2. a business arrangement for the supply of goods or services at a fixed price; 3. a written document that describes the terms of an agreement
B. *contract* \kən-'trakt\ v: 1. to shorten a word by omitting one or more sounds or letters; 2. to make a thing smaller or shorter by pulling it together
C. *contract* \'kän-ˌtrakt\ v: 1. to become ill with a disease

Exercise 5: Word Meanings

Look at the way the word *contract* is used in the following sentences and then, for each sentence, write the letter of the meaning that best fits *contract*. Why did you choose that meaning? Write your reason on the line given.

___ 1. In order to become a club member you must sign a *contract* and pay three months' fees in advance.

Reason: _____

___ 2. Metals expand when heated and *contract* when cooled.

Reason: _____

___ 3. The words "do" and "not" *contract* to form the word "don't."

Reason: _____

___ 4. People traveling in the tropics are advised to take medicine so they will not *contract* malaria and other illnesses.

Reason: _____

___ 5. This *contract* specifies the price and delivery date of each item purchased.

Reason: _____

Understanding Words in Sentences

Exercise 6: Word Meanings in Context

In the reading passages, scan for the words and phrase given in the following list. The number of the paragraph containing the word or phrase is given in parentheses. Circle the letter of the meaning that is most appropriate within the context of the reading passage.

1. rotated around (4)
   a. alternated with
   b. were centered around
   c. went back and forth

2. arbitrarily (6)
   a. according to a plan
   b. by choice
   c. at random

3. revolt (11)
   a. rebelled against
   b. became angry
   c. became upset, disgusted

4. layer (12)
   a. a flat piece of something
   b. a pile of something
   c. a person who lies

5. conceive (15)
   a. to figure out
   b. to become pregnant
   c. to imagine

6. created (16)
   a. thought of
   b. made
   c. developed

Exercise 7: Collocations

Match the verbs with their common collocations by writing the combinations on the lines following the verbs.

a situation	a work of art	a job to someone	a role
problems	homework	when cold	a marriage
what someone says	tuberculosis	a text	

Verbs

1. create

_____

_____

2. assign

_____

_____

3. comprehend

_____

_____

4. contract

_____

_____

Using Words in Communication

Exercise 8: Listening

Listen to the sentences on the audiotape. Then listen again and try to fill in the missing words or phrases. When you are finished, compare your answers to those given in the Answer Key.

1. The singers warmed up for their performance. As I walked down the

   hall I heard _____ voices singing: "Ye, ya, yo, you" and
   "woooo woooo" and "hahaha, hohoho, heeheehee."

2. I thought of my own dance warm-ups. If I wanted to be able to dance

   well I first had to practice. I spent hours _____

   _____ _____ my _____ until they ached.

3. The hotel wasn't large enough, so we had to share rooms. But the

   rooms were not _____ _____. We could each choose
   our own roommates.

4. Mr. Julian said that he would _____ _____

   _____ by sending me his "heart." When I got to my dressing

room a package was waiting for me. Was it really his heart? My

stomach was _____ _____ as I peeled away the

_____ _____ _____ and opened the box. I
was very relieved when I saw that his heart was only a cake!

Exercise 9: Reading and Speaking

Read and answer the following questions. Share your answers with a
classmate.

1. Do you consider yourself a creative person? Why or why not? Give
   examples to support your answer.
2. What is the biggest difference between your native culture and
   American culture? How do you feel about this difference?
3. Have you ever seen a performance (a drama, an opera, a concert) in a
   theater? Describe what you liked most about it. Have you ever
   performed on stage yourself? How did you feel?

Paraphrase

To *paraphrase* is to write or say something in different words but keep
the original meaning. Look at these examples.

1. The singers took no notice of me, but I couldn't do the same with
   them.
   Paraphrase: The singers ignored me, but I couldn't ignore them.

2. He said that if we didn't want to be assigned bed space arbitrarily, we
   should choose our own roommates and let him know.
   Paraphrase: He told us that if we didn't want him to assign our rooms
   at random, we had to choose our own roommates and then tell him
   our choice.

3. But since I believe that God created all things, I know that these
   people are also children of God.
   Paraphrase: Because I believe that God made everything, I know that
   he made these people, too.

Exercise 10: Paraphrasing

Read the sentences given here and then paraphrase them. Use different words in your paraphrase but be sure to keep the original meaning.

A. I unwrapped the package slowly. As I pulled away the last layer of paper I could see that Mr. Julian's "heart" was only a cake!

Paraphrase: _____

_____

B. The noises they made were very loud. The sounds vibrated in my ears.

Paraphrase: _____

_____

C. As I watched the singers perform I felt that they really were the poor Southern blacks whose lives rotated around the work camp of Catfish Row.

Paraphrase: _____

_____

Exercise 11: Writing

Write a two or three paragraph essay that answers one of the questions in Exercise 9.

Unit 5
Cesar Chavez

Vocabulary Preview

Preview 1

Complete each sentence with the most suitable word.

sociologists	issues	goal	primitive	attain

1. Years ago, farmworkers lived in very _____ housing.

2. Cesar Chavez's _____ in life, his mission, was to fight the extreme poverty of migrant farmworkers.

3. It was from the great leader Mahatma Gandhi that Chavez got the idea of using nonviolent means to _____ social justice.

4. Chavez did not have a great deal of faith in _____ who asked a lot of personal questions but never took any action.

5. Ross taught Chavez that _____ did not need to be solved by one person at a time; they could be solved on a group basis.

Preview 2

Look at the way the underlined words are used in the sentences. Match each word with its definition by writing the letter of the correct definition on the line.

1. Chemical sprays are sometimes used to eliminate harmful insects.
2. In 1969, she attained her goal—to become a missionary to Africa.
3. The Hindu calendar, dating back to 1000 B.C., is still used in India to establish the dates of the Hindu religious year.
4. John undertook the huge task of training his staff in modern methods of farming.
5. Paint samples can assist the police in identifying the make and model of a car involved in an accident.

___ 1. eliminate   a. reaches
___ 2. attains   b. try, attempt, endeavor
___ 3. establish   c. help

___ 4. undertake   d. do away with

___ 5. assist   e. set, fix, institute

Reading Preview: What Do You Know about Cesar Chavez?

Circle the correct answer. If you don't know the answer, guess.

1. Cesar Chavez was a
   a. Mexican American
   b. farmworker
   c. union organizer
   d. all of the above

2. A "barrio" is a (an)
   a. neighborhood
   b. bar
   c. office
   d. health clinic

3. A migrant worker is someone who
   a. moves from one area to another planting and gathering crops
   b. stops immigrants from entering the country illegally
   c. helps immigrants get settled in a new country
   d. trains immigrants to do their jobs properly

Adapted from *Cesar Chavez: Autobiography of La Causa* by Jacques E. Levy (New York: W. W. Norton, 1975), 18–19, 35–36, and 73–74, and from *Cesar Chavez: Leader of Migrant Farm Workers* by Doreen Gonzalez (Springfield, N.J.: Enslow Publishers, 1996), 51–57 and 63–65.

Introduction to the Readings

Cesar Chavez, the Hispanic labor leader, was born of immigrant Mexican parents in Yuma, Arizona, in 1927. His name has become synonymous with the struggle of American migrant farmworkers to improve their living and working conditions.

Chavez did not start his life as the son of migrant workers. At the time of his birth, Chavez's parents owned and operated a grocery store and gas station, and initially, Cesar enjoyed a relatively comfortable life with his parents in the apartment above the store. But then the Great Depression came. It was a time in America when many people lost their jobs and their homes. Chavez's father lost his business and was forced to move his family back to his parents' homestead. This land, over one hundred acres, had been owned and farmed by the Chavez family since 1888 and was lost a few years after the Depression began when, unable to pay the taxes, they were forced to sell it. Young Cesar's parents had no choice but to pack their belongings and, as migrant workers, head with their children to the fields to plant and gather crops.

Cesar spent many years going with his family from one area to another, picking fruit and vegetables under the most primitive and oppressive conditions. As a young man he stopped farming the land in order to dedicate his life to bettering the lives of all farmworkers. What was really impressive about his achievement was not only that he built the first successful farmworkers' union in the United States but that he did it without using violent methods.

Using the strike and the boycott as his weapons, Chavez began to wage war against the produce growers by leading a number of nationwide boycotts on fruits and vegetables, most notably the five-year boycott of California table grapes in 1968. By 1970, with millions of Americans supporting the boycotts, Chavez was successful in getting California growers to sign with his newly founded union, the United Farm Workers of America. Eventually, his UFW merged with the national labor union, the **AFL-CIO**.

The excerpts that follow are from Jacques E. Levy's *Cesar Chavez: Autobiography of La Causa* and from Doreen Gonzalez's *Cesar Chavez: Leader for Migrant Farm Workers*.

AFL-CIO: a merger of two powerful unions, the American Federation of Labor, which organized workers according to crafts, and the Congress of Industrial Organization, which organized workers by industries

Reading 1: A Migrant Worker's Life

Migrant workers harvesting onions. Photo by Nell Campbell. Compliments of the Archives of Labor and Urban Affairs, Wayne State University. Reprinted with permission.

(1)   Cesar Chavez spent his childhood and youth following his parents into the fields of California to harvest the crops. Chavez remembers these early years.

(2)   "The crops changed and we kept moving. There was a time for planting and a time for thinning and an endless variety of harvests up and down the state, along the coast and the interior valleys. Some jobs were easy and some very hard, but the worst—a man-killer—was **topping** sugar beets. I was around sixteen or seventeen when I first topped beets in the Sacramento Valley. Those beets grew big, some of them weighing fifteen pounds. The soil, which was almost always clay, was wet and stuck to the beet as it was pulled out of the ground. The skin on my hand would split between the thumb and the index finger as I pulled, and the stooping was always really painful.

(3)   Other hard jobs were thinning lettuce and sugar beets during the winter. Both were just like threads, the plants so small that when I looked at one, there might be ten plants there. They were so close together that all I

---

topping: the term used by farmworkers for removing leaves from the top part of a plant

could do was pull them out by hand . . . Every time I see lettuce now the first thing I think of is that some human being had to thin it. And it's just like being nailed to a cross. You have to walk twisted, as you're bending down, facing the row and walking perpendicular to it. You are always trying to find the best position because you can't walk completely sideways, it's too difficult, and if you turn the other way, you can't thin out the plants."

(4)   Not only were the planting and the harvesting very difficult, the living conditions under which these were undertaken were very bad as well. Growers hiring the migrants were satisfied with providing migrants with "camps": shelters which always turned out to be the only most basic, primitive housing. Cesar recalls:

(5)   "There were hundreds and hundreds of people in these camps, which were huge and almost bare of facilities such as running water and inside bathrooms. Everything was done outside except sleeping, which was in tents. There was no place to do the laundry, just a faucet someplace for providing water for fifty or a hundred families. And the outside toilets were always horrible, so miserable you could not go there."

(6)   Eventually, with the clear goal of fighting extreme poverty, substandard living conditions, exploitation of children, and the obvious discrimination against **Mexican American** migrant workers, Chavez left the fields to organize the workers into the National Farm Workers Association (NFWA). This **union,** organized in 1962, was the first successful union of farmworkers.

(7)   In carrying out his goal, Chavez was always guided above all by his mother's "consejos" or advice. Of his mother, he says:

(8)   "Mother always gave us a lot of consejos . . . She would say, 'El que no coje consejos no llega a viejo' or 'He who does not listen to advice will never grow to be old.' When I look back, I see her advice had a big impact on me. I didn't know it was nonviolence then, but after reading Gandhi and other exponents of nonviolence, I began to clarify that in my mind. Now that I am older, I see my mother was nonviolent, if anybody was, both by what she said and what she did . . . She would always talk about not fighting. Despite a culture where you're not a man if you don't fight back, she would say, 'No, it's best to turn the other cheek. God gave you senses like eyes, and mind, and tongue, and you can get out of anything.' "

Mexican Americans: American citizens whose ancestors immigrated into the United States from Mexico
(labor) union: an organization that looks out for the rights of its members

(9)   Thus, in the manner of his mother, of **Mahatma Gandhi**, and of Martin Luther King, Jr., Chavez held on to the belief, during the early formative years of his union, that the best way to attain victory was through orderly, passive resistance. Rather than encouraging fighting, burning, and destruction, Chavez used the strike and the boycott to get growers to bargain with the union. He sent his union workers to all parts of the country to organize boycotts; that is, to form picket lines and hold signs in front of supermarkets urging consumers not to buy the products of growers who refused to enter into **collective bargaining**. These strikes and boycotts drew nationwide support and eventually ended in the desired result: growers began signing bargaining agreements with the union.

Cesar Chavez speaking with striking farmworkers, c. 1972. Compliments of the Archives of Labor and Urban Affairs, Wayne State University. Reprinted with permission.

Mahatma Gandhi: a leading figure of Indian nationalism who helped his country attain independence through nonviolent means

collective bargaining: the process leading to a formal agreement between employers and labor unions regarding worker rights and benefits

Reading 2: The Training Ground

(10)   Cesar Chavez credited two people with having a significant influence on his life. The first was a Catholic priest, Father Donald McDonnell, who regularly came to his neighborhood to say Mass. Because there were no churches in the barrio, services were held in an old hall that Chavez helped clean and paint. McDonnell was about the same age as Chavez, and it wasn't long before the two were friends.

(11)   During their time together, Chavez and McDonnell talked about farmworkers and their problems. McDonnell understood how large landowners stayed rich by keeping migrant workers in poverty. He showed Chavez photographs of a worker's shack and a grower's mansion and of a migrant camp and a grower's large office building. From these pictures Chavez came to realize the unjust difference between laborers' wages and growers' profits.

(12)   McDonnell also gave Chavez books about outstanding men who were dedicated to helping others. For example, he told him about Mahatma Gandhi. Gandhi (1869–1948) had become internationally famous for leading India to independence from British rule. Gandhi's methods were peaceful but effective. Mostly, he used fasting, group action, and **economic warfare** to fight the English. Yet Gandhi never gave up on his commitment to nonviolence in achieving a goal. Chavez was quick to understand Gandhi's message of attaining social justice through peaceful means. Perhaps this was because Chavez's mother had already given him a firm foundation regarding the value of nonviolence. Chavez would eventually use some of Gandhi's methods himself.

(13)   The second person who greatly influenced Chavez was Fred Ross. Ross had moved to California to create a Community Service Organization, or CSO. This organization's goal was to unite people and give them political power. By the end of six years, Ross had attained his goal—a CSO was firmly established in Los Angeles. By 1952, he was ready to establish CSOs in other urban areas.

(14)   Ross moved to San Jose, where many Mexican Americans lived. One of the first people he met there was Father McDonnell. McDonnell immediately put Ross in contact with Chavez. McDonnell had introduced Chavez to men dedicated to service and nonviolence. Fred Ross took Chavez's education a

economic warfare: Fighting competitors not with weapons but with any method that makes them lose money. Strikes and boycotts are two weapons used to wage economic warfare.

step further. He showed him how to use service and nonviolence to change people's lives. Of Ross, Chavez simply said, "He changed my life."

(15)   In the beginning, however, Chavez had no interest in meeting Ross. When Chavez was told by a friend that Ross was coming to talk to him, he was annoyed. He had spoken with sociologists before who asked personal questions but took no action, and Chavez thought Ross was just another one coming to pry. So on the day that Ross was due to arrive, Chavez walked across the street to his brother Richard's house. When Ross came, Chavez's wife, Helen, told him Chavez was gone. But Ross was persistent. He came back three more times, and the last time Helen refused to lie. Instead, she pointed to Richard's house.

(16)   Still, Chavez meant to have the last word. After Ross talked him into holding a small meeting in his home, Chavez made plans to sabotage the gathering. He invited the roughest men he knew to listen to Ross politely— until Chavez passed his cigarette from one hand to the other. On this signal, the men were to cause as much trouble as possible. But when the meeting started, Chavez was struck by how much Ross knew about his Mexican neighborhood. The arguments he used made sense, and the passion he brought to his mission was evident. Ross showed Chavez that the problems of the poor didn't need to be solved one person at a time. Issues could be attacked on a group basis. The other men watched for Chavez's signal, but it never came. Growing tired of waiting, a few began to give Ross a hard time. Chavez quickly told them to leave, eliminating his original plan.

(17)   At that first meeting, Ross liked Chavez as much as Chavez liked him. He saw immediately that Chavez understood how the oppressed could acquire power. Ross saw, too, that Chavez had the drive to help others gain that power. Ross once said that the people who would change society would be people "who just cannot live with themselves and see injustice in front of them. They must go after it wherever they see it, no matter how much time it takes and no matter how many sleepless nights of worry." Before he went to bed, the night he met Chavez, he wrote in his diary, " I think I have found the man I've been looking for."

(18)   Now after a day's work, Chavez hurried off to other house meetings with Ross, gatherings very much like the ones Chavez had held in his own home. At the meetings, Chavez was quiet, but he watched and listened carefully to every word Ross uttered. Once he was back home, he thought about the things Ross had said and the way the organizer was getting individuals to

work together as a close group. One of the CSO's main goals was getting people registered to vote. Soon Chavez and others volunteered to dedicate some of their evenings and weekends to a voter registration drive in the barrio. Day after day, they canvassed the area, knocking at every door. They talked with people about their personal problems and problems common to the poor. Then they told the people how they could effect change by voting for leaders who would help. Little by little they made people see how important it was to vote. Though the others were casual about the drive, Chavez took it seriously and worked each day. For eighty-five nights in a row he walked the streets, encouraging people to register. His dedication paid off. By the 1952 general election, the CSO had registered four thousand new voters.

(19)   Soon Chavez was spending more and more time working with the CSO. To build a **power base** the vote was crucial. To vote, one had to be an American citizen. Though many Mexicans qualified for citizenship, they had never become official citizens. So Chavez helped them with the necessary paperwork and coached them for their citizenship tests. One thing led to another, and before long Chavez was representing people at places like the doctor's office, the dental clinic, and the local school. Gradually Chavez learned to ask the people he assisted to help the CSO. Of this exchange, Chavez once said, "I was willing to work day and night for people—provided they also did something for the CSO in return."

Comprehension Check

Check your understanding of the reading selections by marking these sentences true (*T*) or false (*F*).

___ 1. Cesar Chavez was born in 1927 in a migrant workers' camp in Yuma, Arizona.
___ 2. When going from one place to another gathering the crops, migrant workers lived in camps provided by the growers.
___ 3. The living conditions in these camps were extremely primitive.
___ 4. Chavez learned from Fred Ross that there is a big difference between a migrant worker's shack and a grower's mansion.

power base: a base of political support

—— 5. Chavez learned from his father that it is always better to turn the other cheek.

—— 6. Chavez learned from Mahatma Gandhi to use peaceful means to attain political power.

—— 7. Chavez established the first successful union of migrant farmworkers in the United States.

—— 8. In building the union, Chavez's most effective tools were strikes and boycotts.

Word Study

 University Word List Vocabulary

assist	establish	primitive
attain	exponent	sociology
community	issues	undertake
crucial	perpendicular	urban
eliminate	persist	voluntary

Understanding Words

Word Relationships

Exercise 1: Synonyms

Select a synonym from the Word List for each underlined word or phrase. Write your choices on the lines.

1. Knowledge about maps is <u>very important</u> in military operations.

   _____

2. The effects of the medicine <u>last</u> for several hours.

   _____

3. Joining the Congress of Interracial Equality was <u>not compulsory</u> for the employees; no one was forced to join.

   _____

4. Flavin was one of the leading <u>believers</u> of using simple, basic forms in creating art.

   _____

5. One of the major goals of international trade agreements is to <u>get rid of</u> any issue that stops nations from selling goods to each other.

   _____

6. Traditionally, American women did not <u>do</u> any work outside the house, but now many women work.

_____

Exercise 2: Compounds

The adjective *urban*, from the Latin *urb* meaning *city*, appears most commonly in compound phrases used in describing or talking about the city. Match each phrase with its definition by writing the letter of the correct definition on the line.

a. the spread of urban houses and businesses out to undeveloped areas near the city
b. construction projects designed to replace poor housing in the cities
c. the dirt, noises, chemicals, and heavy traffic that make some cities unpleasant and unsafe places to live in
d. places where large numbers of people work and live; in other words—cities
e. unattractive areas of the city such as slums or abandoned structures
f. organized efforts to design cities as pleasant and efficient places to live

__ 1. urban pollution
__ 2. urban sprawl
__ 3. urban renewal
__ 4. urban centers
__ 5. urban blight
__ 6. urban planning

Exercise 3: Compounds

Each of the following compound phrases, made up of *community* and another noun, has a specific meaning. Draw a line from each phrase on the left to its meaning.

1. community center
2. community chest
3. community college
4. community property
5. community service
6. community organizer
7. community singing

a. what is owned together by husband and wife
b. a two-year institution usually offering associate degrees
c. a fund obtained from people in the community to give out to people who need help
d. someone who gets people to work together to achieve particular goals
e. a place that offers recreational and educational activities to a neighborhood
f. organized singing by everyone gathered in a particular place
g. the free assistance given by a convicted person to a community in place of serving a jail sentence

The Grammar of Words

Exercise 4: Derivatives

Assistant, a derivative of *assist,* means *someone who helps.* Match each assistant with two job responsibilities by writing the letters of the correct responsibilities on the lines.

__ and __
__ and __
__ and __
__ and __

1. medical assistant
2. dental assistant
3. administrative assistant
4. legal assistant

a. cleaning someone's teeth
b. researching old law cases
c. traveling with employer to meetings and conferences
d. taking someone's temperature
e. summarizing meetings for employer
f. checking out a client's alibi
g. taking someone's blood pressure
h. taking X-rays of teeth

Exercise 5: Derivatives

Complete the chart with derivatives of the italicized words. (Not all blanks can be filled in.)

Noun	Noun (person)	Adjective	Verb
_____	assistant	_____	_____
attainment	_____	_____	
_____	_____	_____	persist
elimination	volunteer	_____	_____
_____	_____	_____	issue

Word Meanings and Forms

Exercise 6: Using Words Correctly

Look up the words *urban, suburbs,* and *suburban* in your dictionary. Write *C* if *urban, suburbs,* or *suburban* is used correctly within the context of the sentence. Write *I* if it is not.

Example: C   Life in the *suburbs* is usually quieter than life in the city.
             I   The *urban* is prettiest in autumn, when the leaves start to fall.

___ 1. *Suburbs* are often called "bedroom communities" because they are places where people return to sleep after working in the city all day.

___ 2. White Plains is a *suburban* of New York City.

___ 3. Traffic is not a major problem in the *suburbs*.

___ 4. *Suburb* shopping centers are very popular with American families.

___ 5. The instructions read: "Do not take the train into the city; get off at *Suburban* Station."

___ 6. An *urban* renewal project will start in that part of the city next week.

Exercise 7: Word Meanings

Where are you likely to find the following—in urban centers or in the suburbs? Write the items on the lines under the appropriate headings.

museums   swimming pools   vegetable gardens
parking lots   trees and flowers   office buildings

Urban Centers   *Suburbs*

_____   _____

_____   _____

_____   _____

Exercise 8: Word Meanings

What do people with these jobs do? What does the suffix *-ist* mean? Write your definitions on the lines. Use your dictionary if necessary.

Example: A *sociologist* is someone who *studies how groups of people live and behave.*

1. A *psychologist* is someone who _____.

2. An *economist* is someone who _____.

3. *Impressionists* were nineteenth-century painters who _____.

4. An *archaeologist* is someone who _____.

Exercise 9: Word Meanings

A perpendicular line is one that is always at right angles to another line. Parallel lines are lines that are always at the same distance from each other and that never meet.

   In the box on the left, draw lines that are perpendicular to each other.
   In the box on the right, draw lines that are parallel to each other.

Understanding Words in Sentences

Exercise 10: Word Meanings in Context

Reread the following passages from the text. Then complete the sentences or answer the questions by circling the letter of the correct choice.

1. You have to walk twisted, as you are stooped over, facing the row and walking perpendicular to it. You are always trying to find the best position because you can't walk completely sideways, it's too difficult.

   To thin the lettuce, Chavez had to walk
   a. at a right angle to it
   b. parallel to it
   c. at a little distance from it
   d. one foot away from it

2. Not only were the planting and the harvesting very hard but the living conditions under which these were undertaken were horrible as well.

   Undertaken here means
   a. agreed upon
   b. rejected
   c. embraced
   d. done, attempted

3. Growers hiring the migrants were content with providing them only with camps, shelters that always turned out to be the most primitive living accommodations.

   In the camps, the migrants
   a. were provided with good food and housing
   b. had the most terrible, inadequate kind of housing
   c. were provided with housing but not with food
   d. were always guaranteed running water

4. Thus, in the manner of his mother, of Mahatma Gandhi, and of Martin Luther King, Jr., Chavez held on to the belief, during the early formative years of his union, that the best way to attain victory was through orderly, passive resistance.

Chavez held on to the belief that
a. the best way to win was through peaceful means
b. the best way to win was to organize people
c. the best way to win was through organized fighting
d. the best way to win was to develop good leaders

5. Ross was just as impressed with Chavez at this first meeting as Chavez was with him.

What was Ross's first impression of Chavez?
a. He doubted whether he would be a good organizer.
b. He liked him very much.
c. He was worried about his communication skills.
d. He thought his accent would be a problem.

Exercise 11: Collocations

Underline the words and phrases in this paragraph that are associated with or collocate with *organizing a drive to get people to vote*. Share your list with another student.

Soon Chavez and others volunteered to dedicate some of their evenings and weekends to a voter registration drive in the barrio. Day after day, they canvassed the area, knocking at every door. They talked with people about their personal problems and problems common to the poor. Then they told the people how they could effect change by voting for leaders who would help. Little by little they made people see how important it was to vote. Though the others were casual about the drive, Chavez took it seriously and worked each day. For eighty-five nights in a row he walked the streets, encouraging people to register. His dedication paid off. By the 1952 general election, the CSO had registered four thousand new voters.

Exercise 12: Constructing Sentences

Use the set of words to ask a question. (No additional words are needed.)

1. exponent/passive resistance?/most/of/was/the/Who/famous

   _____

2. was/In/the/rewarded?/his/end,/persistence

   _____

3. like?/What/migrant/camps/worker/were

   _____

4. his/establish/first/Where/Ross/did/CSO?

   _____

5. best/could/to/be/According/how/issues/Ross/attacked?

   _____

Using Words in Communication

Exercise 13: Speaking

With another student, take turns asking and answering the following questions.

1. Once he left the fields, what mission did Chavez undertake?
2. What kind of voluntary work was done by Chavez initially?
3. What did Chavez accomplish as a community organizer?
4. Who assisted Chavez in registering people to vote?
5. Who established the first union of farmworkers? What was it called?

Exercise 14: Writing

Use this information to write a short biographical essay on Cesar Chavez.

born on March 31, 1927, in Yuma, Arizona
child of Mexican American migrant farmworkers
lived in a succession of migrant camps
attended school occasionally
joined the Navy and served for two years
became a community organizer and, eventually, general director of CSO
left CSO to found the National Farm Workers Association
led many strikes and boycotts against growers
strikes and boycotts were successful and generally ended with the
    signing of bargaining agreements
recognized today as organizer and leader of migrant American
    farmworkers

Unit 6
Gloria Steinem

Vocabulary Preview

Preview 1

Complete each sentence with the most suitable word.

mental   income   consulted   concentrate   transformation

1. No one wondered about my mother's _____. To relatives, this new Ruth was simply a sad event.
2. No one asked if my mother's suffering might be due to her medicine.

   No one even _____ another doctor about it.

3. We lived off the _____ that my mother got from renting out her land.

4. The family assumed that _____ illness was just part of her personality.

5. She could rarely _____ long enough to read a book.

Preview 2

Look at the way the underlined words are used in the sentences. Match each word with its definition by writing the letter of the correct definition on the line.

1. People cannot drink pure alcohol, but they do drink beverages like beer or wine that contain alcohol.
2. Although Tim Gullikson was a great tennis player, he was best known as the coach who guided the career of Pete Sampras.
3. In addition to writing popular suspense stories, Edgar Allan Poe worked as a magazine editor.
4. Scientists believe that, over millions of years, all animals evolved from single-celled organisms.
5. The death of a child is a very depressing event. Most parents feel terrible sadness and loss for years afterward.

___ 1. alcohol
___ 2. career
___ 3. edit
___ 4. evolve
___ 5. depressing

a. causing feelings of sadness, disappointment, loss
b. a chemical substance found in beer or wine
c. a longtime job or profession
d. to develop or change over time
e. to examine and correct a piece of writing

Reading Preview: What Do You Know about Gloria Steinem?

Circle the correct answer. If you don't know the answer, guess.

1. Gloria Steinem
   a. attended Harvard University
   b. started *Ms. Magazine* in 1972
   c. was president of Smith College
   d. developed new drugs to treat mental illness

2. Gloria Steinem is best known
   a. for her work on women's issues and human rights
   b. for her work with the mentally ill
   c. for her work on the environment
   d. for her work in education

3. In America in the 1940s and '50s
   a. mental illness was generally ignored
   b. there were no treatments for mental illness
   c. mentally ill people were often put into hospitals or given drugs
   d. mental illness was very common

"Ruth's Song (Because She Could Not Sing It)" Adapted from *Outrageous Acts and Everyday Rebellions,* by Gloria Steinem (New York: Henry Holt and Co., 1983), 139–58.

4. Women in America in the 1940s and '50s
    a. were expected to marry and have children
    b. were expected to have their own careers
    c. usually kept working after they married and had children
    d. got divorced if they were not happy in their marriages

Introduction to the Reading

Gloria Steinem is one of the most influential woman writers, editors, and **political activists** of our time. Born in 1934, Gloria Steinem began writing shortly after graduating from Smith College in 1956. The following year she traveled to India and worked with followers of Mahatma Gandhi. The trip to India influenced Steinem greatly and was the beginning of her work as a nonviolent political activist. Steinem is probably best known as an editor of the **feminist** *Ms. Magazine,* an international magazine devoted to women's issues, which she founded in 1972. **Ms.** Steinem also works worldwide for other causes related to inequality and women's rights.

Ms. magazine cover, 5th Anniversary Issue, July 1977. Reprinted by permission of *Ms.* magazine, © 1977.

political activist: a person who actively promotes a political cause
feminist: a person who works to promote women's rights and issues; a person who supports political, economic, and social equality for women
Ms.: a title like "Mr." that can be used by both married and single women; the name of the feminist magazine Gloria Steinem founded

The excerpt here comes from the essay "Ruth's Song (Because She Could Not Sing It)," published in *Outrageous Acts and Everyday Rebellions* in 1983. In this essay, Steinem writes about her mentally ill mother, Ruth, and their life together.

Reading: "Ruth's Song (Because She Could Not Sing It)"

(1)   Happy, or unhappy, families are all mysterious. The question is: Why are some mysteries more important than others?

(2)   For many years I couldn't imagine my mother, Ruth, any way other than the way she was when I was born. She was just a fact of life when I was growing up. She was someone to be worried about and cared for; someone who lay in bed with her eyes closed and lips moving in response to voices only she could hear. She was a woman to whom I brought endless amounts of toast and coffee, sandwiches and pie, in a child's version of what meals should be. She was a loving, intelligent, and terrorized woman who tried hard to clean our house whenever she emerged from her private world but who rarely finished a task. In many ways our roles were reversed: I was the mother and she was the child.

(3)   I suppose I must have known that years before I was born, my mother had been different. She had been an energetic, adventurous young woman who struggled out of a **working class family** and into college and who had a career. She loved her job and continued it even after she was married and had my older sister to care for. The family must have watched this energetic woman, who loved books and fun, turn into someone who was afraid to be alone. She became a woman who could not **hang onto reality** long enough to have a job and who could rarely concentrate long enough to read a book.

(4)   Yet I don't remember my family wondering about the mystery of my mother's transformation. To the kind relatives, this new Ruth was simply a sad event. She was a family problem to be accepted and cared for until some natural process made her better. To the less kind relatives and those who envied her earlier independence, my mother was a woman who wanted to

---

working class family: a family whose members work at manual labor or other jobs that do not require a college education

hang onto reality: be aware of the real world; function in the real, normal world

fail. She was someone who lived in a dirty house, a woman who simply refused to **pull herself together.**

(5)   Outside events were never suggested as reason enough for her problems. Giving up her own career was never seen as a cause for her depression. Even the explanation of mental illness made it seem like it was all my mother's fault. She had suffered her first "**nervous breakdown**" before I was born, when my sister was about five. This breakdown followed years of trying to take care of a baby, be the wife of a kind, but financially irresponsible man, and still keep her job as a reporter and newspaper editor. After many months in a mental hospital, she was pronounced "cured." That is, she was able to take care of my sister again and to move away from the city. She left the job she loved and worked with my father at an isolated, rural **vacation resort** in Michigan.

(6)   But she was never again completely without the times of depression, anxiety, and **visions into some other world** that eventually turned her into the "nonperson" I remember. And she was never again without a bottle of dark, bad-smelling medicine—**tranquilizers** that the doctor gave her. Our friends and relatives always saw this medicine as more evidence of my mother's weakness. To me it always seemed an embarrassing but necessary evil. It made her speech difficult to understand, and she became physically awkward. Our neighbors and my school friends believed she was a drunk. But without the medicine she would not sleep for days, even a week at a time. Then her tired eyes would begin to see only a private world where wars and angry voices threatened the people she loved. It is no wonder that no relative ever challenged the doctor who gave my mother this medicine. No one asked if some of my mother's suffering and the visions she saw might be due to the drugs. No one even consulted another doctor about its use. The medicine was our relief as well as hers.

(7)   But why was she never taken back to that first hospital? Or taken to other doctors for help? Partly, it was her own fear of returning to that pain. Partly, it was too little money and the family's assumption that mental illness was just a part of her personality. Looking back on it, perhaps the biggest reason my

---

pull herself together: to control herself; to be in control of her actions
nervous breakdown: An illness where a person has deep depression, worry, and tiredness. This kind of illness might be treated with rest, drugs, or counseling.
vacation resort: A place where people go to take a vacation. This resort was in the state of Michigan, in the northern central part of the United States.
visions into some other world: Gloria's mother saw things that did not really exist.
tranquilizers: drugs that make people feel less anxious and nervous

mother was cared for but not helped for twenty years was the simplest: my mother's functioning was not that necessary to the world. She was like the women alcoholics who drink in their kitchens while male executives who drink get expensive care. She was like the homemakers who are calmed with drugs while male patients get therapy and personal attention instead. My mother was not an important worker.

(8)   My father kept our household going until I was eight or so and my sister went away to college. Then I replaced my father. I did not blame him for leaving us once I was old enough to bring meals and answer my mother's questions. That's why our lives, my mother's from forty-six to fifty-three and my own from ten to seventeen, were spent alone together. Most of those years we lived in a house in Toledo, Ohio. We lived off the tiny **fixed income** that my mother got from renting out her share of the land in Michigan.

(9)   In that house, I remember

. . . lying in the bed my mother and I shared, listening to the early morning live radio broadcast of the royal wedding of Princess Elizabeth and Prince Phillip.

. . . hanging paper curtains I had bought in the **dime store.** I piled books and papers in the shape of two armchairs and covered them with blankets. I evolved my own dishwashing system—I waited until all the dishes were dirty, then put them in the bathtub. And then I listened to my mother's praise for my housekeeping efforts.

. . . on a hot summer night being bitten by one of the rats that lived in our house and the street behind it. It was a terrifying night that turned into a touching one. That night my mother, getting courage from her love for me, became a calm, comforting parent who took me to a **hospital emergency room** in spite of her terror of leaving home.

fixed income: The amount of money that Gloria's mother got regularly from renting her land. This amount of money never got larger or smaller; it stayed the same.
dime store: a store that sells many inexpensive things
hospital emergency room: the place in hospitals where you can get immediate medical treatment, without an appointment

. . . coming home from the local library with the books I would escape into and discovering that, for once, there was no need to escape. My mother was calmly planting flower seeds in the **empty lot** next door.

(10)   Later, when I was finishing high school, my father took my mother with him to California for a year. Suddenly I was far away from her, in Washington, living with my sister. Then I could afford to think about the sadness of my mother's life. I realized that as a child my sister had known a very different person who lived inside our mother, an earlier Ruth.

(11)   This Ruth was a person I met for the first time when my mother was in a mental hospital near Baltimore, after my sister had had the courage to get her the help she needed. At first, this Ruth was the same frightened woman I had lived with all those years. But gradually she began to talk about her past life and to share her memories. I began to meet a Ruth I had never known.

. . . a tall, energetic, red-haired high school girl who loved basketball and reading. A girl who tried to drive her uncle's car when it was the first car in the neighborhood. A girl who had a gift for gardening and who sometimes wore her father's overalls!

. . . a good student at **Oberlin College,** whose traditions she loved. A student with a talent for mathematics and poetry. A daughter who had to return to Toledo, live with her family, and go to a local university when her mother—who had lived cheaply and saved, worked, and made her daughters' clothes in order to have money to send them to college—ran out of money.

. . . a daughter who became a **part-time bookkeeper** in a shop, going to classes and listening to her mother's lectures. She was also a young woman who was rebellious enough to fall in love with my father. My father was the editor of the university newspaper, a funny and charming young man who was **unacceptably Jewish.**

---

empty lot: an area of land in a town that is vacant and has no buildings on it
Oberlin College: a prestigious liberal arts college in Ohio; the first U.S. college to admit women
part-time bookkeeper: a person who works less than forty hours a week doing accounting and other paperwork for a business
unacceptably Jewish: Ruth's family was not Jewish and did not want Ruth to marry a Jewish man. To her family, it was not acceptable for Ruth to have a Jewish husband.

(12)   I know from family stories that my mother had married my father twice. They married once, secretly, and once a year later in a public ceremony, which some members of both families had refused to attend because it was a "**mixed marriage.**" And I also know that my mother had gone on to earn a teaching certificate and had taught college mathematics for a year. After graduating from the university, she wrote a newspaper column. Soon after that she got a job as a reporter for one of **Toledo's** big daily papers— eventually she earned the prestigious position of Sunday editor.

(13)   It was a strange experience to look into those brown eyes I had seen so often and realize suddenly how much they were like my own. For the first time I realized that she really was my mother. I began to think about the pressures that might have led up to her first nervous breakdown: leaving my sister at home with our grandmother; trying to keep a job she loved but that my father asked her to leave; wanting to go to New York to pursue her own dream of writing but punishing herself for even thinking about it. She was convinced that divorce was impossible. A husband could not be left for a career. A daughter could not be deprived of her father.

(14)   At the hospital, and later, when my mother told me stories of her past, I used to say, "But why didn't you leave? Why didn't you take the job in New York?" She would insist that it didn't matter, she was lucky to have my sister and me. Sometimes she would add, "If I'd left, you never would have been born." I always thought but never had the courage to say: *But you might have been born instead.*

(15)   I'd like to tell you that this story has a happy ending. The best I can do is an ending that is happier than its beginning. After many months in that Baltimore hospital my mother lived on her own in a small apartment near my sister. When she felt the old terrors coming back, she returned to the hospital at her own request. She was approaching sixty by the time she emerged from the hospital, and in fact, she never returned to it again. She had some independent life and many friends. She worked part-time in a shop. She went away with me on vacation every year and took one trip to Europe with relatives. She went to women's club meetings. She found a **multiracial** church that she loved and attended most Sundays. She took meditation courses and enjoyed many books. Once out of the hospital for good she continued to show flashes of a different woman inside. This other woman had

mixed marriage: a marriage between people of different religious or ethnic backgrounds
Toledo: a city in Ohio
multiracial: containing people of different races and skin colors

a **dry kind of humor,** a sense of adventure, and a love of learning. She died just before her eighty-second birthday.

(16)   I still don't understand why so many years passed before I saw my mother as a person and before I understood that many of the things that happened in her life were patterns that women share. Like a lot of daughters, I couldn't admit that what had happened to my mother was not all personal or accidental. Such things could happen to me.

(17)   So the world missed a unique person named Ruth. Though she dreamed of living in New York and traveling in Europe, she became a woman who was afraid to take the bus across town. Though she drove the first car in her neighborhood, she married a man who wouldn't let her drive at all. I can only guess what she might have become. There were clues in her moments of spirit and humor.

(18)   I miss her. But perhaps I miss her no more since her death than I did during her life. Dying seems less sad than having lived too little. But at least we're now asking questions about all the Ruths in all our family mysteries. If her song inspires that, I think she would be the first to say: It was worth the singing.

Comprehension Check

Check your understanding of the reading selection by marking these sentences true (*T*) or false (*F*).

—   1. When Gloria was a child she took care of her mother, Ruth.
—   2. Ruth came from a wealthy, upper-class family.
—   3. Relatives thought that Ruth's mental illness was her own fault and that she could get better if she tried to.
—   4. Ruth needed to take tranquilizers to sleep, but the medicine had some bad side-effects.
—   5. Gloria lived with different relatives from ages ten to seventeen.
—   6. Ruth was a good cook and housekeeper.

dry kind of humor: humor that is ironic or sarcastic

___ 7. Ruth had been a normal, active young woman until she had a nervous breakdown.

___ 8. Ruth's family was very happy when she married a Jewish man.

___ 9. Gloria thought that her mother's mental illness was a result of the social and family pressures that many women experience.

___ 10. Gloria's mother had started a career as a writer and an editor.

Word Study

 University Word List Vocabulary

alcohol	drug	mental
career	edit	nervous
concentrate	evolve	reverse
consult	finance	tiny
depress	income	transform

Understanding Words

Word Parts

The prefix *trans-* comes from the Latin *trans* and means *across, beyond, through,* or *so as to change.* It is used to form many English words. Each of the following words is a combination of *trans-* and other word parts of Latin origin.

	Prefix	*Root*
transfer	trans- +	ferre (to carry)
translate	trans- +	latus (to change from)
transport	trans- +	portare (to carry)
transform	trans- +	formare (to form)
transmit	trans- +	mittere (to send)

Exercise 1: Prefixes

Complete each of the sentences with the correct word. Add word endings if necessary.

transfer	translate	transport	transform	transmit

1. The United Nations employs highly skilled interpreters and

    _____ to ensure clear communication between delegates
    from different countries.

2. Trucks have replaced trains as the most efficient way of

    _____ goods across the country.

3. Televisions and radios both pick up signals that are _____
    from one point to another.

4. In frogs the _____ from tadpole to adult frog takes place in
    several weeks.

Word Relationships

Exercise 2: Antonyms

Draw a line between each word on the left and its antonym. Use your
dictionary if necessary.

1. concentrate	maximum
2. depressed	huge
3. income	expand
4. tiny	forward
5. reverse	dilute
6. minimum	economy
7. contract	produce
8. consume	elated
9. luxury	expense

Analogies

Remember that an *analogy* shows how two things are related in some
way. Look at these examples.

1. cat : kitten :: dog : puppy
   "Dog" is related to "puppy" in the same way that "cat" is related to
   "kitten."

The first word in each pair is what we call the adult animal; the second word is what we call the young animal.

2. kitten : puppy :: cat : dog

   "Kitten" and "puppy" are both a type of young animal.

   "Cat" and "dog" are what we call the adult types of these animals.

As the examples show, some sets of words may form more than one analogy.

Exercise 3: Analogies

Make an analogy from each group of four words and write it on the blank line below the four words—remember, more than one analogy may be possible. Then describe the relationship that exists in your analogy.

1. alcohol   bread   food   drug

   _____

   relationship: _____

2. nervous   relaxed   tense   calm

   _____

   relationship: _____

3. advise   ask   tell   consult

   _____

   relationship: _____

4. write   editor   edit   author

   _____

   relationship: _____

Exercise 4: Associations

Which topic is each of these words associated with? Write each of the words under the appropriate topic. Add one more word to each list.

alcohol	consult	depressed	drug
evolve	finance	income	mental
nervous	reverse	transform	economy

Health	*Money*	*Emotions*	*Change*
_____	_____	_____	_____
_____	_____	_____	_____
_____	_____	_____	_____
_____	_____	_____	_____

Understanding Words in Sentences

Exercise 5: Word Meanings in Context

Reread the following passages from the text. Then complete the sentences or answer the questions by circling the letter of the correct choice.

1. I began to think about the pressures that might have led up to my mother's first nervous breakdown: leaving my sister at home with our grandmother; trying to keep a job she loved but that my father asked her to leave; wanting to go to New York to pursue her own dream of writing but punishing herself for even thinking about it. She was convinced that divorce was impossible. A husband could not be left for a career.

   Which of these is NOT given as a reason for Ruth's nervous breakdown?
   a. trying to keep a job that her husband wanted her to leave
   b. getting a divorce
   c. giving up her dream of going to New York to write

2. At the hospital, and later, when Ruth told me stories of her past, I used to say, "But why didn't you leave? Why didn't you take the job in New York?" She would insist that it didn't matter, she was lucky to have my sister and me. Sometimes she would add, "If I'd left, you never would have been born." I always thought but never had the courage to say: *But you might have been born instead.*

Gloria thinks that her mother
a. was lucky to have had two daughters
b. didn't really want to work in New York
c. should have taken the job in New York

3. Perhaps the biggest reason my mother was cared for but not helped for twenty years was the simplest: my mother's functioning was not that necessary to the world. She was like the women alcoholics who drink in their kitchens while male executives who drink get expensive care. She was like the homemakers who are calmed with drugs while male patients get therapy and personal attention instead. My mother was not an important worker.

Maybe the biggest reason Gloria's mother was not helped was because
a. her mother did not do any work that was considered important
b. her mother drank
c. her mother was not an executive

4. She was also a young woman who was rebellious enough to fall in love with my father. My father was the editor of the university newspaper, a funny and charming young man who was unacceptably Jewish. I know from family stories that my mother had married my father twice. They married once, secretly, and once a year later in a public ceremony, which some members of both families had refused to attend because it was a "mixed marriage."

Why didn't some family members attend the second wedding?
a. Family members had attended the first wedding.
b. The families didn't approve of a Jewish man marrying a non-Jewish woman.
c. Family members were not invited to the second wedding.

Using Words in Communication

Exercise 6: Listening

Listen to the texts on the audiotape until you understand them. Then circle the correct answers.

1. What kind of career did Ruth have?
   a. She was an engineer.
   b. She was a college teacher.
   c. She was a newspaper editor.

2. When did Gloria first hear about her mother's past life?
   a. while they were living together
   b. when her mother was in a mental hospital
   c. when Ruth was frightened

3. Ruth had
   a. been a talented, intelligent young woman
   b. been very bad at mathematics
   c. never liked writing

Exercise 7: Speaking

In the reading Ruth is described as a normal young person and later as a person who is mentally ill. Working by yourself, write down all the words you can think of that are related to Ruth in each situation. When you are finished, share your answers with a classmate. Some words are given to help you get started.

1. *Ruth as a Normal Young Person*

intelligent _____

fun _____

_____

_____

_____

2. *Ruth When She Is Mentally Ill*

can't concentrate _____

nervous _____

_____

_____

_____

Exercise 8: Speaking

Think about these questions and then discuss your answers with a classmate. Next, choose one of these topics and prepare a three- to five-minute presentation to give in class.

1. According to this reading, what kind of role, or position, do you think women were expected to have in American society 50 years ago?
2. What kind of roles were women expected to have in your country 50 years ago? Compare this with the situation in America 50 years ago.
3. What kind of roles do you think young men and women expect to have today? How is this different from what their fathers and mothers expected? Give examples from your own life if you want to.

Exercise 9: Reading

Read the text that follows and fill in the blanks with one of these words or phrases. Then answer the questions.

medication	drug	very nervous	consult
chemical	therapy	depressant	function normally
anxiety	bodies	brain	mental condition

A Common Anxiety Disorder

About twenty-three million people in the United States have _____s called "anxiety disorders." One type of anxiety disorder is called "agoraphobia." The term *agoraphobia* comes from the Greek words *agora*, meaning *marketplace*, and *phobia* meaning *a fear of something*. When a person has

agoraphobia he or she feels _____ and afraid when out in open public places or in crowds of people. Some people may actually feel so nervous that they completely stop going out and remain at home all the time. When they do go out, people with agoraphobia often

experience "panic attacks." During a panic attack their _____ react as if they were in extreme danger: their hearts beat very fast, they sweat, and they feel knots in their stomachs and lumps in their throats.

Today there are two types of treatment for these _____ disorders. The first is cognitive therapy. During cognitive therapy the person learns how to accept his or her fear and function in spite of it. The person may also learn relaxation and breathing techniques or have some type of "talking"

_____ with a counselor.

The second type of treatment is medication. A person's tendency toward panic attacks and the severity of his or her symptoms may be affected by

levels of certain _____s in his or her _____.

There are many drugs that can be used to help these conditions. Anti

_____ drugs and antianxiety drugs are used more than tranquilizers because these drugs are not habit forming. Some people

need to take _____s long term; others only take them temporarily.

Doctors usually combine cognitive therapy with _____.

The goal is to help the person recover and _____ again. If you know a person who experiences severe panic attacks or agora-

phobia please urge him or her to _____ a doctor. Help is available.

Questions

1. Give one example of an anxiety disorder. What happens when a person has this condition?

   _____

   _____

2. Do you think that you would see a person with agoraphobia at the shopping mall or at a football game? Explain why.

   _____

   _____

3. Give at least two ways a doctor might treat a person with this type of anxiety disorder.

_____

_____

4. Do you know what these phobias are?

claustrophobia: _____

acrophobia: _____

Can you name any other phobias?

_____

Exercise 10: Writing

Choose one of the following topics and write a two or three paragraph essay.

1. Gloria Steinem's childhood was very different from the life most children have. Compare her childhood to yours.
2. In the first paragraph of the reading Gloria writes that "all families are mysterious." Are there any mysteries, or mysterious people, in your family? Describe the mysterious situation or person as clearly as possible.

Review Unit 2

I. Choose the correct word from the list on the left to go with each meaning. (In each set, you will not use two of the words.)

Set A

    1. arbitrary   __ to make more difficult
    2. assist   __ to set up, to institute
    3. complicate   __ at random, not considering the results
    4. establish
    5. edit

Set B

    1. adjust   __ one who promotes a cause
    2. attain   __ to get used to, to correct
    3. transform   __ to change or alter
    4. exponent
    5. drug

Set C

    1. comprehend   __ to change over time
    2. volunteer   __ a matter in dispute
    3. quote   __ freely offer to perform a service or task
    4. issue
    5. evolve

II. Choose an antonym for each word on the right. (In each set, you will not use two of the words.)

Set A

1. approach
2. eliminate
3. legal
4. primitive
5. drama

— advanced
— criminal
— add

Set B

1. reverse
2. urban
3. terror
4. crucial
5. perpendicular

— forward
— rural
— unnecessary

III. Match each word on the left with a common collocation by writing the letter of the correct choice on the line.

— 1. layer
— 2. nervous
— 3. luxury
— 4. alcoholic
— 5. community
— 6. contract
— 7. minimum
— 8. income

a. automobile
b. center
c. rental
d. wage
e. fixed
f. cake
g. beverage
h. habit
i. primitive
j. site

IV. Match each word on the left with its synonym by writing the letter of the correct synonym on the line. (You will not use one synonym.)

— 1. rotate
— 2. comprehend
— 3. site
— 4. revolt
— 5. undertake

a. rebel
b. turn
c. create
d. understand
e. attempt
f. location

V. Complete the analogies that follow with one of the words given here.

huge	groups	mind	choice
ill	city	nervous	concept

1. small : large :: tiny : _____

2. rural : country :: urban : _____

3. biology : life :: psychology : _____

4. crucial : need :: optional : _____

5. mental : depressed :: physical : _____

VI. Complete each sentence with one of the words given here. You may need to change the form of the word or add word endings.

overlap	sociology	finance	rotate
concept	muscle	income	mental

1. The singers' voices _____ and harmonized as they sang the final song together.

2. _____ is the study of how groups of people live and behave.

3. Students may go to the _____ aid office for help in obtaining grants, loans, and scholarships.

4. In some primitive societies, the _____ of private property does not exist.

5. To build _____ the body requires adequate food, especially protein, and regular exercise.

Unit 7
Georgia O'Keeffe

Vocabulary Preview

Preview 1

Complete each sentence with the most suitable word.

abstraction   method   elements   superior   create

1. Georgia thought that colors were _____ to the English language for communicating her feelings about something.
2. Dow had students balance their compositions by adding or

    eliminating _____ and changing the positions of shapes.
3. Bement encouraged his art students to _____ pleasing and unusual patterns of their own.

4. The Dow _____ resulted in dull student work, and it was abandoned after Dow's death in 1922.
5. Looking through Dow's textbooks, Georgia absorbed lessons about

    the principles of _____.

Preview 2

Look at the way the underlined words are used in the sentences. Match each word with its definition by writing the letter of the correct definition on the line.

1. Music critics must understand the musical works that they write about.
2. World famous opera, ballet, and theater enrich the cultural life of New York City.
3. A square is a special kind of rectangle with four sides of equal length.
4. Her sketches showed ideas for a painting that she was planning to do.

5. Number <u>theory</u> is the branch of mathematics that explains the properties of whole numbers (1, 2, 3, 4, 5, . . .).

___ 1. critic	a. a rough, simple drawing
___ 2. enrich	b. a shape that has four sides
___ 3. rectangle	c. an idea that attempts to explain something
___ 4. sketch	d. a person who evaluates something
___ 5. theory	e. to improve by adding to

Reading Preview: What Do You Know about Georgia O'Keeffe?

Circle the correct answer. If you don't know the answer, guess.

1. Georgia O'Keeffe was
   a. a famous fashion designer
   b. an art critic
   c. a twentieth-century painter
   d. the first professional woman photographer

2. Georgia O'Keeffe is well known for
   a. her use of unusual black and white fabrics
   b. the use of brilliant colors in her paintings
   c. her black and white photographs
   d. her reviews of famous art exhibits

3. Georgia O'Keeffe died
   a. very young
   b. an unknown artist
   c. after a long illness
   d. nearly blind at the age of 98

Adapted from *Portrait of an Artist: A Biography of Georgia O'Keeffe* by Laurie Lisle (New York: Washington Square Press, 1986), 57–59, 79–82, 346–48, 350–53.

Introduction to the Readings

Georgia O'Keeffe is considered the most important American woman painter of this century. She was born in 1887 and died in 1986, living and painting in Abiquiu, New Mexico, for most of her 98 years. O'Keeffe's art was original in its style and subject matter. Her brilliantly colored paintings of bold, **sensuous** flowers, and **sun-bleached** animal bones are still well liked today. The excerpts that follow are adapted from Laurie Lisle's book: *Portrait of an Artist: A Biography of Georgia O'Keeffe.*

The first excerpt, "Arthur Wesley Dow's Teachings," describes Georgia's early artistic education at the University of Virginia. In the second excerpt, "An Important Decision," Georgia recalls her "breakthrough" into her own unique and feminine style of artistic expression. The final excerpt, "Thinking in Colors," explains how Georgia used color, and her art, as a way to communicate the ideas she wanted to express.

Reading 1: Arthur Wesley Dow's Teachings

(1)   In the summer of 1912 Georgia's sister, Anita, signed up for summer school courses at the University of Virginia. Drawing was taught by a professor who, Anita quickly decided, had unusual ideas about art. Georgia had given up art, but Anita told Georgia that she was sure she would be interested in the class. So Georgia went to art class with her, although in a highly doubtful frame of mind.

(2)   Georgia and Anita walked into the classroom. The course was "Drawing I," a class usually taken by elementary school teachers. The instructor was Alon Bement, a thirty-seven-year-old man, who was assistant professor of fine arts at Columbia University Teachers College in New York. Bement was also a friend of Arthur Wesley Dow, the head of the fine arts department at Teachers College. Dow's way of teaching art was quietly revolutionary. Unlike the instruction at most art schools, his method had little to do with copying nature or the styles of the **old Masters**. Dow had devised exercises that

sensuous: something that appeals to the senses
sun-bleached: whitened by exposure to the sun
old Masters: famous European painters from the thirteenth to seventeenth centuries; painters like Rembrandt, Van Dyke, and Botticelli

enabled people who weren't artists, even those who couldn't draw, **to master** the principles of design. Dow's exercises included dividing a square, working within a circle, enclosing a drawing with a rectangle, and then balancing the composition by adding or eliminating elements and changing the positions of shapes.

(3)   As Bement encouraged his students to create pleasing and unusual patterns of their own, Georgia looked and listened carefully. In most cases, the Dow method resulted in dull student work, and the method was abandoned after Dow's death in 1922. But for Georgia this method suddenly provided an intellectual foundation for art. Looking through Dow's textbooks, *Composition* and *The Theory and Practice of Teaching Art,* Georgia absorbed lessons about the ideas of beauty that underlie paintings and the principles of abstraction. The Dow method was a step beyond the realistic art that seemed to have no purpose to Georgia. It was also comprehensive. Georgia later said that Dow's idea was very simple but it could be used to make every artistic decision. It also provided a kind of "alphabet" that could be arranged and rearranged and resulted in a great deal of individualism. "It seemed like equipment to go to work with," Georgia recalled. "Art could be a thing of your own."

(4)   The next morning, Georgia returned to the university. She signed up for Bement's most advanced class, "Drawing IV," which met late each weekday afternoon during the six-week summer session.

Reading 2: An Important Decision

(5)   Seven years later, Georgia recalled the breakthrough she had experienced in her art. At that time art still represented the freedom of expression that it had when she was a teenager.

I grew up pretty much as everybody else grows up. One day seven years ago I found myself saying: I can't live where I want to, I can't go where I want to, I can't even say what I want to. School and things that painters have taught me even keep me from painting as I want to. I decided that I

---

to master (something): to learn something well and become skillful at it was a very stupid fool not to at least paint as I wanted to and say what I wanted to when I painted. That seemed to be the only thing I could do that didn't concern anybody but myself. My painting was nobody's business but my own.

(6)   Georgia put all her old artwork away in order to clear her mind completely of the influence of others. She also put away her watercolor paints, not wanting to have to think about colors. She decided to work only in black and white until she exhausted all their possibilities. At the age of twenty-seven she started all over again, in the simplest way: drawing with charcoal. "It was like learning to walk again," she remembered.

(7)   Every night she spread rough student sketch paper on her bedroom floor and sat on the floor. She worked, rubbing the paper with charcoal, until her body ached and the charcoal fell apart in her fingers. Sometimes she wondered whether the abstract shapes that she saw in her mind meant that she was crazy. (This was a reasonable idea since both creativity and insanity have been linked to the ability to see reality differently.) Those weeks were a high point in Georgia's life that she would always try to recreate. "I was alone and free, working into my own unknown, with no one to satisfy but myself," she recalled.

(8)   Later, people who looked at those abstract drawings saw violent, explosive emotions, driven by sexual energy. This energy seemed to threaten to tear the artist apart. Sharp edges pushed against soft forms. Moving shapes jumped up like flames reaching for oxygen. One of the drawings showed volcano-like shapes erupting with fire and steam, which Georgia had visualized during one of her then frequent headaches.

(9)   Georgia clearly knew that she was revealing a female feeling. "The thing expresses in a way what I wanted it to, but it also seems rather feminine. It is essentially a woman's feeling. It satisfies me in a way," she told a friend. However, a few years later, when male art critics began to emphasize this sexual point, Georgia rejected their comments on the subject. She thought they were exaggerating.

Reading 3: Thinking in Colors

(10)   Georgia thought in color the way other people thought in words. She joked that she hoped to give up reading and writing with the help of the telephone, tape recorder, and radio. In spite of the fact that Georgia had an expressive and distinctive writing style, she said that words were often false, meaningless, and limited. On the other hand, color was something she could trust. It was a world in which new variations could still be found.

(11)   Georgia thought that her color vocabulary—of colors ranging from shiny blacks to airy white—was superior to the English language. Because of this she often refused to talk about her work and was reluctant to try to describe it in words. "I see no reason for painting anything that can be put into any other form just as well," she once said. She explained that she preferred to paint her feeling about something rather than to talk about it. She used to tell frustrated interviewers that she didn't like to think in words. Words were too stiff and unbending.

(12)   Once when someone asked Georgia why she painted skulls, she said that she was unable to explain it in words and would have to paint a picture to explain it. "Probably I would do a picture with another skull in it and then where would we be?" she asked with a little smile. Sometimes her sense of humor left her entirely. "The meaning is there on the canvas, "she said angrily to an art critic. "If you don't **get it**, that's too bad. I have nothing more to say than what I painted."

(13)   Georgia's natural way of communicating was to place lines, shapes, symbols, and colors together so they spoke eloquently. Her genius lay in her ability to create an artistic "language" that translated her intense feelings. When Georgia explored the vibrations of the color blue, for instance, she could awaken feelings in viewers with her **cobalt blue tones**. She could lead their imaginations into "almost unknown relationships with life," as Blanche Martin said in 1926. It was clear that O'Keeffe's skillful use of shapes and symbols, which was constantly enriched by her fertile imagination, could confront the viewer's senses on a gut or emotional level. This was the reason Georgia disliked it when her symbols were explained, because this lessened a painting's **emotional impact**.

get it: slang for "understand it"
cobalt blue tone: a strong, dark blue color
emotional impact: emotional force; the effect something has on the emotions or feelings

Jimson Weed (1932) by Georgia O'Keeffe. Oil on canvas. 48 × 40 inches. Copyright The Georgia O'Keeffe Museum. Reprinted with permission.

Comprehension Check

Check your understanding of the reading selections by marking these sentences true (*T*) or false (*F*).

___ 1. The Dow method did not impress Georgia O'Keeffe.
___ 2. Georgia was frustrated by her early artistic education because it did not allow her to paint the way she wanted to.
___ 3. At twenty-seven, Georgia taught herself to draw again using only black and white.
___ 4. Art critics claimed that Georgia O'Keeffe's artwork was sexual in a feminine way.
___ 5. Georgia was a poor writer.
___ 6. Georgia enjoyed explaining her art to people.
___ 7. Toward the end of her life Georgia suffered a mental breakdown.

Word Study

 ## University Word List Vocabulary

abstract	fertile	reveal
critic	individual	sketch
design	intellect	superior
element	method	theory
enrich	rectangle	visual

Understanding Words

Word Parts

Exercise 1: Prefixes

The prefixes *in-* and *un-* mean *not*. Add the correct prefix meaning *not* to each word and write the new word on the line. Write a short definition of the new word. (Use your dictionary if you need to.)

1. aware _____

   definition: _____

2. critical _____

   definition: _____

3. expert _____

   definition: _____

4. fertile _____

   definition: _____

5. reliable _____

   definition: _____

Exercise 2: Suffixes

The suffixes *-ity, -tion,* and *-ation* are added to adjectives or verbs to form nouns. The suffix *-ity* means *state of being,* and the suffixes *-tion* and *-ation* mean *the act or state of . . .*

Add *-ity, -tion,* or *-ation* to the words given here. Some words may have two forms. Then fill in the blanks in the following sentences with the appropriate new words.

abstract _____   conform _____

visualize _____   confront _____

fertile _____   devote _____

1. Diplomats met day and night in order to prevent a serious

   _____ between the two countries.

2. Dogs are considered "man's best friend" because of their

   _____ to their owners.

3. _____ rates are dropping among people who live in industrialized countries; most couples have only one or two children.

4. The technique of _____, imagining something before actually doing it, helps many athletes perform better.

5. The priest was a serious man who always lived in strict

   _____ with his religious beliefs.

Word Relationships

Exercise 3: Synonyms

Cross out the word in each series that is not a synonym for the first word in that series. Use your dictionary if necessary.

1. enrich	wealth	enhance	improve	supplement
2. fertile	rich	pregnant	fruitful	productive
3. intellect	reason	thought	emotion	intelligence
4. reveal	show	cover	uncover	tell

5. superior	better	equal	over	greater
6. element	part	substance	quality	group
7. method	culture	way	technique	procedure
8. theory	belief	question	principle	hypothesis
9. design	plan	purpose	pattern	method

Understanding Words in Sentences

Exercise 4: Word Meanings in Context

In the reading passages, scan for the words given in the following list. The number of the paragraph containing the word is given in parentheses. Circle the letter of the meaning that is most appropriate within the context of the reading passage.

1. design (2)
   a. a plan for making something
   b. an arrangement of artistic elements
   c. a detailed drawing

2. elements (2)
   a. shapes
   b. parts
   c. borders

3. abstraction (3)
   a. realistic art
   b. art based on numbers
   c. art that is not realistic

4. individualism (3)
   a. something unique, personal
   b. something similar
   c. something copied

5. sketch (7)
   a. a drawing on paper
   b. used for drawing
   c. draw quickly and simply

6. visualized (8)
   a. looked at
   b. dreamt about
   c. saw in her mind

7. revealing (9)
   a. showing
   b. baring, uncovering
   c. feeling

8. critic (12)
   a. a report or evaluation
   b. a person who evaluates
   c. a thing that is essential

Exercise 5: Word Meanings in Context

Find the words in the text that have the following meanings and write these words on the lines provided. The number in parentheses is the number of the paragraph where the word occurs.

1. made it possible to do something (2) _____

2. to make, imagine, or invent (3) _____

3. to stand for, symbolize (5) _____

4. not peaceful, forceful, painful (8) _____

5. womanly, feminine (9) _____

6. to stress, to indicate strongly (9) _____

7. untrue (10) _____

8. unique, easily recognizable (10) _____

Exercise 6: Words in Context

Complete each sentence using one of the words from the following list. Change the word form by adding -s, -ed, or -ing if necessary.

abstract	fertile	rectangle	sketch
enrich	individual	reveal	visual

1. Most processed foods have been _____ with vitamins and minerals.

2. Each student will have his or her own _____ identification number and e-mail address.

3. Music is not a _____ art, but painting and sculpture are.

4. The Napa River valley is an excellent area for farming: the soil is

   _____, and the weather is perfect for growing many types of crops.

5. In the planning phase the designer will do many rough _____ before drawing the final design.

6. His diaries _____ many things that were not known about his personal life.

Exercise 7: Collocations

Match items 1 through 8 with their common collocations by writing the combinations on the lines following items 1 through 8.

theory   element   arts
design   product   land
method   idea

1. production

_____

_____

2. basic

_____

_____

3. sophisticated

_____

_____

4. scientific

_____

_____

5. abstract

_____

_____

6. visual

_____

_____

7. fertile

_____

_____

8. superior

_____

_____

Exercise 8: Collocations

Write these phrases on the lines next to the verbs they collocate with. Then write down two more words that are commonly used with each verb.

a policy	a product	a secret	a picture
a plan	an idea	a view	the meaning
an essay	a building	an outline	the ending

Verbs

1. sketch

_____

_____

_____

_____

_____

2. reveal

_____

_____

_____

_____

3. criticize

_____

_____

_____

_____

4. design

_____

_____

_____

_____

Using Words in Communication

Exercise 9: Listening

Listen to each text on the audiotape and then summarize it in two or
three sentences. Try to use at least one study word in your summary.

1. _____

    _____

2. _____

    _____

3. _____

    _____

4. _____

    _____

Exercise 10: Discussion

Working in pairs, discuss the following questions.

1. Why do you think that Georgia felt she could express herself better
   by painting than by using the English language? Do you agree or
   disagree with Georgia? Give examples from your own life to support
   your opinion.
2. Think of two famous artists. What type of art is each of them famous
   for? Why do you think these artists are famous? Is their art abstract
   or realistic?
3. Think about photography, architecture, music, and dance. Do you
   consider these types of "art"? Why or why not? In your opinion,
   what is "art"?

Exercise 11: Discussion

Bring an example of art to class. (This can be a picture from a magazine
or newspaper, a postcard, a photograph, etc.) Bring an example of art
that you like *or* an example of art that you dislike.

Then study the following questions. Think of how you will answer these questions about your example. Talk to your classmates about their examples and get answers to these questions.

1. Who made your piece of art?
2. What medium (materials) did the artist use?
3. Where was this made?
4. When was this made?
5. What do you like or dislike about your art?
6. What do you think the artist was trying to express?

Exercise 12: Read and Understand the Text

Work together with other students. Use these words to fill in the blanks in this reading passage. Then answer the questions.

visual	sketch	method	individual
design	element	superior	rectangle
critically	enrich	reveal	theory

Unpainted Shapes

(1)   When I ask students, "What is the strongest _____ in a painting?" the usual answers are _____ technical ability, a strong _____, and an _____ artistic style. Students never think of the simplest element of all—leaving white paper white. A little investigation will _____ that the eye quickly picks out shapes of plain white paper. Areas left white reflect light or "glow" more than dark or heavily painted areas which do not reflect much light. As a result, your eye will go to these glowing light areas first.

(2)   Because of this luminous, glowing quality, white paper has the same _____ power as a heavy, dark color. To understand this idea, try a simple experiment. Paint a black circle in a white square or _____.

Adapted from *Making Color Sing* by Jean Dobie; p. 114. Copyright 1986 by Jean Dobie, Watson-Guptill Publications (Billboard Publications, Inc., 1515 Broadway, NY, NY 10036).

Next to that, paint another square but reverse the colors: paint a white circle within a black square. (It is important to keep both circles the same size in order to compare them fairly!) Now, notice how the white circle appears to expand. Also, notice how your eye is drawn to the white circle more than the black one.

(3)   When you create a design the white shapes in it must function as part of

the painting. I suggest that you draw out your ideas on _____ paper. Draw the white, unpainted areas as well as the painted ones. Then paint all of the areas of the sketch that will be white in the final painting with

black paint. This _____ will give you an "X-ray" of your design that can help you see where it may be unbalanced or weak. When you are finished

painting, step back and look _____ at the black and white shapes.

Are they strong? Does each shape _____ the overall design?

1. What word or phrase in paragraph 1 means *sees* or *notices*?

   _____

2. What word or phrase in paragraph 2 means *grow* or *become larger*?

   _____

3. What word or phrase in paragraph 3 means *act as* or *work as*?

   _____

Exercise 13: Read and Outline

Read this text that describes the process Georgia followed when she painted a picture. Next, outline the process that Georgia goes through as she paints an abstract painting. Finally, describe her paintings. Be sure to include all important information.

(1)   Georgia's painting methods developed early. Although she was not the type of artist who goes into the studio each day to paint, she did prepare for the moment when she would feel ready to begin. She stretched canvases and primed them with a white undercoat—several individual blank canvases were usually ready for use in her studio.

(2)   She learned to wait during the weeks or months it took for a design to form in her mind. "I know what I'm going to do before I begin, and if there's

nothing in my head, I do nothing," she explained. Her ideas came in various ways. "I have the kind of mind that sees these shapes—many come from realistic or natural bases, but others are just beautiful shapes that I visualize in my mind."

(3)   By the time Georgia began to paint a canvas it was basically a matter of methodically putting down the elements already in her head. Generally she made a preparatory sketch, then mixed her paints and placed them on her palette. She painted rapidly, pausing only to eat, and usually she was finished with a small canvas by the time the daylight faded.

(4)   From girlhood on Georgia had done paintings in a series. As she went along she simplified the image so that it lost its resemblance to the original object. "Nothing is less real than realism. Details are confusing. It is only by selection, by elimination and by emphasis that the real meaning of things is revealed." The last picture in a series was often just her concept of the subject's core. O'Keeffe said, "It can be nothing but abstract, but it is my reason for painting, I suppose."

Exercise 14: Writing

You are an art critic who writes reviews of art for a magazine or newspaper. Find a book with pictures of art or go to an art gallery or a museum to look at some art. Choose a piece of art and look at it carefully. Write a two or three paragraph "review" that describes the art you chose and your feelings about it. Look back at Exercise 11 for things you may want to include in your review. Share your review with other students.

Unit 8
Carl Sagan

Vocabulary Preview

Preview 1

Complete each sentence with the most suitable word.

constructed   diagram   reactions   planets   technology

1. At the top left is a _____ of the neutral hydrogen atom.

2. However, such _____ were quite rare, and in general, the nude drawings produced no great protest.

3. I realized how far away _____ must be to appear as tiny points of light in the sky.

4. At the World's Fair I saw a vision of a perfect future made possible by science and high _____.

5. The ship was artificially _____; it was not a natural object.

Preview 2

Look at the way the underlined words are used in the sentences. Match each word with its definition by writing the letter of the correct definition on the line.

1. "Cloning" human cells to produce human beings is a controversial idea. People have very different opinions about it.
2. These diagrams illustrate how costs have increased over the past ten years.
3. Intelligence tests are designed to measure the ability to make abstractions, to learn, and to deal with new situations.
4. The principle of inertia states that an object at rest will tend to remain at rest unless acted upon by an outside force.
5. The Sun affects the Earth through its ultraviolet radiation and the solar wind.

___ 1. controversial   a. a general scientific law
___ 2. illustrate   b. the ability to think, understand, and learn
___ 3. intelligence   c. causing many different strong feelings
___ 4. principle   d. having to do with the Sun
___ 5. solar   e. show, depict

Reading Preview: What Do You Know about Carl Sagan?

Circle the correct answer. If you don't know the answer, guess.

1. Carl Sagan
   a. was the first man to walk on the moon
   b. was a mathematician
   c. worked with Albert Einstein
   d. was an astronomer, a writer, and a teacher

2. Which one of these statements would Carl Sagan *disagree* with?
   a. Intelligent life may exist on other planets.
   b. Science should be explained so that everyone can understand it.
   c. Ordinary people don't need to understand science.
   d. It is important to spend money on scientific research.

3. The Pioneer 10 space project
   a. sent an unmanned spaceship to Mars
   b. was never completed because it was too expensive
   c. caught the public's attention because of the plaque Sagan designed for it
   d. was a joint project between the United States and Russia

4. Carl Sagan
   a. is a professor at Cornell University
   b. died of cancer at the age of 62
   c. died in the space shuttle "Challenger" accident
   d. continues to write science fiction stories

Adapted from *The Demon-Haunted World* by Carl Sagan (New York: Random House, 1996, xiii–iv and 25–26, and *Carl Sagan: Superstar Scientist* by Daniel Cohen (New York: Dodd, Mead and Co., 1987), 40–47.

Introduction to the Readings

Carl Sagan was born in 1934, in Brooklyn, New York. His love for science and astronomy started at the age of five, when his parents took him to the **1939 New York World's Fair**. This love for science helped Sagan become one of the most well-known scientists, writers, and teachers of the "**space age.**" His interest in space exploration and the possibility of finding life on other planets led to his work on many space projects. Carl Sagan was also known for his ability to explain science and make it exciting to ordinary people. His television series *Cosmos* was seen by more than five hundred million people, and his novel *Contact* was made into a popular movie in 1997. Sadly, Carl Sagan died of cancer in 1996.

In the first excerpt, adapted from his book *The Demon-Haunted World*, Sagan describes his feelings about science and its importance in our lives. The second excerpt, from Daniel Cohen's book *Carl Sagan: Superstar Scientist*, explains Sagan's interesting and unusual contribution to the **Pioneer 10 space project**.

Reading 1: A Love Affair with Science

(1)   I was a child in a time of hope. I wanted to be a scientist from my earliest school days. I wanted to be a scientist from when I first understood that the stars are huge suns and when I first realized how far away planets must be to appear as tiny points of light in the sky. I'm not sure I even understood the meaning of the word *science* then, but I wanted to somehow involve myself in all that. I felt the wonder of the universe. I looked forward to understanding how things really work, to helping uncover deep mysteries, and to exploring new worlds. I have been fortunate to have had part of my dream fulfilled.

(2)   For me, science remains as appealing and new as it was on that day, more than half a century ago, when my parents showed me the wonders of the 1939 New York World's Fair. At the fair I saw a vision of a perfect future

1939 New York World's Fair: The 1939 World's Fair was held in New York. The theme of this World's Fair was "The World of Tomorrow."
space age: the late twentieth century, after World War II, when countries like the United States and the former Soviet Union began to explore space
Pioneer 10 space project: an unmanned spaceship, launched by NASA in 1972, to collect information about the area of our solar system near Jupiter

made possible by science and high technology. The "World of Tomorrow" would be sleek, clean, and streamlined. As far as I could tell, it would also be without a trace of poor people.

(3)   "See sound," one poster commanded. And, sure enough, when a **tuning fork** was struck by a little hammer, a beautiful wave moved across a screen. "Hear light," another poster said. And sure enough, when a light shone on a **photoelectric cell**, I could hear something like the noise on our radio when it was set between stations. Obviously the world held wonders of a kind I had never guessed. How *could* a sound become a picture and light become a noise?

(4)   I wish I could tell you about inspirational science teachers from my elementary, junior high, or high school days. But as I think back on it, there were none. It wasn't until college that I finally found teachers who were able to explain science. Many things that had been mysterious to me became clearer, and I felt the joy of discovering a little about how the universe works. After that, I had a strong desire to "popularize" science. I wanted to try to make its methods and **findings** accessible to people who aren't scientists. Not explaining science so that ordinary people can understand it seems very strange to me. When you're in love you want to tell the world. I've had **a love affair with science** my whole life.

(5)   But there's another reason I want to popularize science. Science is more than a body of knowledge; it is a way of thinking. I can imagine an America, in my children's or grandchildren's time, when nearly all the key manufacturing industries have moved to other countries and the United States is a service and information economy. I can imagine a time when huge technological powers are in the hands of a very few and no one representing the **public interest** can even understand the issues; when ordinary people have lost the ability to determine what they really want or to intelligently question those in authority. A time when, **holding our crystals and nervously consulting our horoscopes,** our ability to think critically in decline, we are unable to

tuning fork: A small tool with a handle and two prongs that makes a particular tone when struck. It is used for tuning musical instruments.
photoelectric cell: When light shines on this device, an electrical current is produced.
findings: the results or conclusions of research
a love affair with science: to love science with the kind of passion that you feel in a love affair
public interest: a topic or concern that affects all the members of a community; for example schools, roads, or taxes
holding our crystals and nervously consulting our horoscopes: Sagan is talking about people who rely on superstitious things, such as crystals, horoscopes, fortune-tellers, and so on, in order to make decisions about their lives.

distinguish between what feels good and what is true. I can imagine a time when we slide, almost without noticing, back into superstition and darkness.

(6)   The "**dumbing down**" of America is most evident now in the slow decay of the content of the media, the 30-second sound bites (now down to 10 seconds or less) and the TV and radio programming aimed at the lowest possible level. It is evident in the shows that present **pseudoscience** and superstition as real facts, and it is especially evident in a kind of celebration of ignorance. As I write, the number-one video cassette rental in America is called *Dumb and Dumber.* A TV show called *Beavis and Butthead* is very popular (and influential) with young television viewers. The plain lesson here is that study and learning—not just of science but of anything—are things that we should avoid.

(7)   We have made a global civilization in which most crucial elements: transportation, communications, the industries of agriculture, medicine, education, entertainment, and protecting the environment all depend on science and technology. Even the key democratic institution of voting depends on science and technology. And we have also arranged things so that almost no one understands science and technology. This is a formula for disaster. We might **get away with it** for a while, but sooner or later this dangerous mixture of ignorance and power is going to blow up in our faces.

Reading 2: The Pioneer 10 Project

(8)   One of Carl Sagan's projects will last longer than the pyramids. It will last longer than any other current artifact. Some people have commented that it may well outlast the human race itself. Nothing better illustrates Sagan's boldness and his talent for getting the public's interest and attention than the small golden plaque attached to the Pioneer 10 spaceship.

(9)   Pioneer 10 itself was a very bold project. It was conceived and carried out in the early 1970s, a time of active scientific space research. The Pioneer spaceship was designed to explore the environment in the outer **solar system**, primarily the huge planet Jupiter. The ship was not designed to send

dumbing down: the simplification of something so that it is very easy to understand
pseudoscience: "Pseudo-" means false. Pseudoscience is when something that cannot be proven by experiments and research is called "science."
get away with it: be able to do something successfully that can't or shouldn't be done
solar system: a sun and all of the planets and comets that orbit around it

back any messages from beyond the solar system, and it was not specifically aimed at the **planetary system** of any nearby star. After completing its job, Pioneer 10 would travel silently in space for hundreds of millions of years.

(10)   What if this wandering spaceship were found by an advanced **extraterrestrial** civilization? What would they think of it? The extraterrestrials would probably be able to recognize the ship as an artificially constructed rather than a natural object. But they would have no way of knowing where Pioneer came from, and they would know nothing about its makers.

(11)   When Sagan first heard that Pioneer 10 was to leave the solar system, he conceived an ambitious plan. Why not put some sort of message on the spaceship so that any **aliens** who might find it would have some chance of answering basic questions about where the ship came from and who sent it? Sagan immediately contacted the National Aeronautics and Space Administration (**NASA**). To Sagan's surprise and delight, the message project was quickly approved.

(12)   The next step was deciding what sort of message to send. How do you attempt to communicate with a theoretical extraterrestrial intelligence that you know nothing about? Obviously an alien is not likely to understand English or any other language from Earth. The message, said Sagan, had to be written in the only language that could possibly be universal: the language of science. Sagan felt that the message should, first of all, convey certain basic scientific principles that should be known to all intelligent beings. This information would prove that the senders of the message were also intelligent.

(13)   The basic message was written in just a few hours. Says Sagan, "At the top left is a diagram of the transition between parallel and antiparallel proton and electron spins of the neutral hydrogen atom. Under this diagram is the binary number 1. Transitions of this type have a known characteristic distance and characteristic time. Since hydrogen is the most common atom in the galaxy, and the laws of physics are the same everywhere in the galaxy, we think that an advanced civilization will have no difficulty understanding this part of the message." Even though most people reading about this diagram cannot understand it, Sagan believed that a civilization advanced enough to capture the Pioneer spaceship in deep space would also contain some individuals who would be able to interpret this diagram.

planetary system: the group of planets that orbit around a star
extraterrestrial: a living thing that lives someplace other than the Earth
aliens: beings from another planet; extraterrestrials
NASA: The National Aeronautics and Space Administration is an independent agency of the United States government, established in 1958 for the exploration of space.

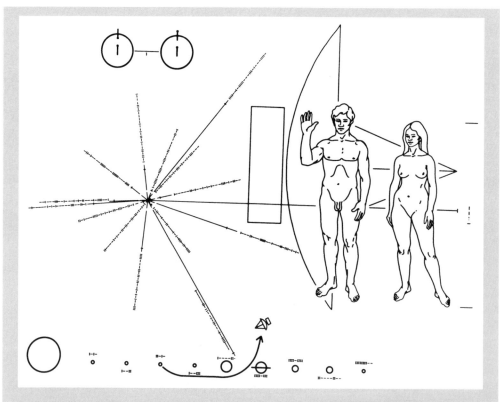

Pictorial plaque carried onboard Pioneer 10 spacecraft. Compliments of National Aeronautics and Space Administration. Reprinted with permission.

(14)   Much of the rest of the message on the plaque tried to communicate when and where the spaceship had been launched. It attempts to show our solar system in relation to fourteen powerful stars that are important features of our galaxy. "The beings who find the message must ask themselves not only *where* it was possible to see fourteen stars in such a position, but also *when* it was possible to see them." The answers are: from one star in **the Milky Way**, our own sun, and from a single year in the history of the galaxy, the year the spaceship was launched. Underneath this is also a diagram of our solar system.

(15)   In addition to the scientific side of the message, an additional human touch was added. The message included a drawing of two nude human figures, male and female. These drawings became the most familiar, and the most controversial, part of the entire Pioneer message project. The message

the Milky Way: the name of the galaxy to which Earth belongs

was put on a six-inch by nine-inch gold and aluminum plate and attached to the spaceship.

(16)   Sagan's "message to the stars" drew public attention in the most extraordinary way. Pictures of the message plaque appeared in newspapers and magazines throughout the world. When the *Los Angeles Times* showed the plaque on the front page it received an angry letter complaining about **"sexual exploitation."** However, such reactions were quite rare, and in general, the nude drawings produced no great protest.

(17)   One thing about the drawings that Sagan felt badly about was that, in our multiracial world, the figures looked distinctly white. It wasn't meant to be that way. "We had hoped to represent at least three of the major races of humankind." The woman was to have a partly Asian appearance, but since her hair was drawn only in outline, she looks like a blonde. In the original sketch the man was drawn with African facial features and short **"Afro" style hair**, but in the final picture he has wavy hair. To Sagan's disappointment, the figures were not as representative of the diversity of the human race as he had hoped they would be.

(18)   There were other criticisms. Why did the man have his right hand raised? On Earth, Sagan said, this is a universal sign of peace. But someone suggested that this gesture looked like a **Nazi salute** and that aliens might conclude that the message was from an unfriendly, evil society. Some women complained that while the male figure was giving the greeting, the female figure wasn't doing anything. She was just standing there with her hands at her sides. A few fearful people even wondered whether this message might tell hostile extraterrestrials where we were. Sagan doubted if this was much of a danger, since our radio and television signals had already been traveling out into space for many years.

(19)   There were a few technical criticisms from the scientific community as well, but generally, scientists and nonscientists alike responded enthusiastically to this unusual project. Suddenly the possibility of actually communicating with other intelligent beings became real and thinkable.

(20)   Sagan knew that the chances of the message of the Pioneer 10 space-

---

sexual exploitation: In this case, the writer felt that the newspaper printed the nude drawings on the front page in order to sell more newspapers; the paper was using sex to make money.

"Afro" style hair: a naturally curly hairstyle, often worn by black people

Nazi salute: A salute with one arm extended up and to the front. This salute was used by the Nazis before and during World War II.

ship actually reaching some beings that could understand it were very unlikely. He referred to the project as "good fun." The real reason for the message, he said, was not out among the stars but back here on Earth. The purpose of the Pioneer 10 message was to encourage us humans to **consider ourselves in a more cosmic perspective**.

Comprehension Check

Check your understanding of the reading selections by marking these sentences true (*T*) or false (*F*).

___ 1. Carl Sagan was very impressed by the 1939 New York World's Fair.

___ 2. Carl Sagan loved science because of the good science teachers he had in junior high and high school.

___ 3. Sagan feels that it is dangerous when most people living in a technological society cannot understand science.

___ 4. Carl Sagan thinks programs like *Dumb and Dumber* and *Beavis and Butthead* teach young people good lessons.

___ 5. Science is important because it teaches people how to think.

___ 6. Pioneer 10 was the spaceship that explored the area around Jupiter.

___ 7. NASA asked Carl Sagan to develop a way to contact aliens.

___ 8. Scientific diagrams were the best "language" to use on the Pioneer 10 plaque because aliens probably can't understand Earth languages.

___ 9. Carl Sagan was pleased with the final plaque because the drawings on it represented many races of people.

___ 10. Carl Sagan believed that extraterrestrial beings would find and understand the Pioneer 10 plaque.

consider ourselves in a more cosmic perspective: Sagan wanted humans to think of themselves as belonging to a huge universe that may contain other intelligent beings.

Word Study

University Word List Vocabulary

communicate	environment	principle
construct	illustrate	project
contact	intelligent	reaction
controversial	interpret	solar
diagram	planet	technology

Understanding Words

Word Parts

Exercise 1: Prefixes

The word *extraterrestrial* appears in paragraph 10 of the reading. If the prefix *extra-* means *outside, except,* or *beyond,* the root *terra* means *earth,* and the suffix *-ial* means *of* or *relating to,* what do you think *extraterrestrial* means?

_____

Look at the way the underlined words are used in the sentences below. Then match each word with its definition by writing the letter of the correct definition on the line.

1. Carl Sagan had an <u>extraordinary</u> passion for science.
2. The Rolls Royce and the Mercedes are <u>extravagant</u> cars compared to a Mustang or a Volkswagen.
3. The most popular <u>extracurricular</u> activities on campus are intramural sports and the drama and music clubs.
4. If you have <u>extrasensory</u> perception you might be able to read people's minds or predict future events.

___ 1. extraordinary
___ 2. extravagant
___ 3. extracurricular
___ 4. extrasensory

a. outside of the 5 senses
b. beyond what is usual, exceptional
c. unreasonably expensive
d. organized student activities that do not carry academic credit

Exercise 2: Suffixes

The suffix -*ology* means *the study or knowledge of . . .*
Combine each of these word stems with -*ology* to form a new word. Write the meaning of the new word. Use your dictionary if necessary.

word stem + -*ology* = new word

1. bio + ology = _____

   meaning: _____

2. techno + ology = _____

   meaning: _____

3. astro + ology = _____

   meaning: _____

4. psycho + ology = _____

   meaning: _____

5. socio + ology = _____

   meaning: _____

Word Meanings and Forms

Read the definitions for the word *project* given here.

A. *project* \'prä-jekt\ n: 1. a scheme or idea; 2. a planned task, often done by students; 3. a carefully thought out piece of research
B. *project* \'prä-jekt\ n: 1. a public housing development, usually consisting of identical houses or apartments
C. *project* \prə-'jekt\ v: 1. to plan, figure, or estimate for the future; 2. to throw forward or stick out; 3. to display or show; 4. to cause an image to fall onto a surface

Exercise 3

Look at the way the word *project* is used in the following sentences and then write the letter of the meaning that best fits *project* in each sentence. Why did you choose that meaning? Write your reason on the line given.

___ 1. Good leaders always *project* an image of strength and confidence, even during times of crisis.

Reason: _____

___ 2. Many of the poorest children in America do not live in inner city *projects* but in small, rural towns.

Reason: _____

___ 3. The *projected* sales for the Mustang's first year were much lower than the number of cars actually sold.

Reason: _____

___ 4. One of Carl Sagan's most interesting *projects,* the plaque attached to the Pioneer 10 spacecraft, will probably last longer than the pyramids.

Reason: _____

___ 5. The roof of the building *projects* out beyond the top of the wall by 12 inches.

Reason: _____

Exercise 4: Word Forms

Complete each sentence with the correct word.

1. In the 1990s _____ weapons, such as those used in "germ" warfare, became as great a threat to human safety as nuclear weapons.
   biologist   biology   bionic   biological

2. Modern medical _____ helps people to live longer, healthier lives.
   technologist   technology   technical   technological

3. In 1962 John Glenn became the first man to orbit the earth; now at age 77, he will also be the oldest _____ to ever travel in space.
   astronaut   astrology   astrological   astronomy

4. Maya Lin was "interested in the _____ of the client," because this helped her to understand the type of design that would appeal to him or her.
   psychologist   psychology   psychic   psychological

5. _____ animals, like dogs and horses, prefer to live in groups, while solitary animals, like the tiger, prefer to live alone.
   sociologist   sociology   social   society

Understanding Words in Sentences

Exercise 5: Word Meanings in Context

In the reading passages, scan for the words and phrase given in the following list. The number of the paragraph containing the word or phrase is given in parentheses. Circle the letter of the meaning that is most appropriate within the context of the reading passage.

1. popularize (4)
   a. become popular
   b. to support something
   c. to make people interested in something

2. body (5)
   a. an organized group of people
   b. a mass of something
   c. the physical parts of a person or thing

3. think critically (5)
   a. analyze and evaluate fairly
   b. judge unfavorably or too severely
   c. think badly of

4. illustrates (8)
   a. draws
   b. shows
   c. pictures

5. environment (9)
   a. physical surroundings
   b. nature and the outdoors
   c. social and cultural conditions

6. conceived (11)
   a. became pregnant
   b. imagined or believed
   c. thought of and planned

7. interpret (13)
   a. translate into another language
   b. understand the meaning or significance of a thing
   c. to stop or cut off

8. rare (16)
   a. infrequent
   b. good or remarkable
   c. valuable, expensive

Exercise 6: Usage

Read each sentence carefully. Write C if the underlined word is used correctly and I if the word is used incorrectly. If a word is used incorrectly, replace it with a better word by writing the new word on the long line.

—— 1. The international conference was held to discuss serious <u>environment</u> issues like global warming and deforestation. _____

—— 2. Public <u>reaction</u> to the new memorial was mixed; half of the people liked it and half hated it. _____

—— 3. Sagan hoped that humans might someday <u>contract</u> intelligent beings from another part of the universe. _____

—— 4. The Earth is one of nine planets in our <u>solar</u> system.

_____

—— 5. Georgia O'Keeffe used the basic <u>principals</u> of design, which she learned from Dow and Bement, as the foundation for her art.

_____

Exercise 7: Collocations

Many words in English commonly collocate with certain prepositions. (Prepositions are words like *about, at, in, for, of, to,* and *with*). However, a word may collocate with more than one preposition; the context determines which preposition is used.

Find these words, or a form of each word, in the reading; underline each word and the preposition it collocates with in this context. The number of the paragraph where a form of the word occurs is in parentheses. Then write the preposition on the line.

1. vision (2) _____

2. desire (4) _____

3. ability (5) _____

4. formula (7) _____

5. communicate (12) _____

6. diagram (13) _____

7. relation (14) _____

8. complain (16) _____

9. respond (19) _____

10. refer (20) _____

Exercise 8: Usage

Look at each of the following sentences. Is anything in the sentence incorrect? If so, cross out the incorrect word. Is anything missing from the sentence? If so, put a caret mark (^) where a word needs to be

added and write in the correct word from the list that follows. The first
sentence has been done for you.

about   for   of   to   with

                    to

1. Public reaction ~~about~~ the drawings was minimal.
2. People from different cultures may have trouble communicating.
3. When called on, the student responded about the correct answer.
4. The young actor had a strong desire of money and fame.
5. The formula on the chemical compound is in your textbook.
6. Their vision to the future did not include poor people.
7. Roberto's pitch ability to was tremendous.
8. Please refer back to the table on page 39.
9. Who is that man in relation of you? Is he your uncle?
10. This diagram for the planets explains our solar system.

Using Words in Communication

Exercise 9: Role Play

Work with another student. One of you will take part A, and one of you
will take part B. Read your part and then make a list of questions you
want to ask your partner. Take turns asking and answering questions.

A. You are an astronaut from Earth. Your mission is to explore planet X,
an unknown planet near our solar system. After your spaceship
lands on the planet, you leave your ship. You are met by a being
from this planet. The being seems friendly and wants to
communicate with you. It can speak your language.

1. What things do you want to know about this planet and its
people?
2. What things will you need to know in order to survive in this new
environment?
3. What would you like to tell this being about Earth and its people?

B. You are a being from the planet X, just outside of the Earth's solar system. A strange-looking metal object has just landed outside your house. You go outside and are surprised to see a shiny silver being with a helmet on its head walking toward you. This visitor seems friendly and wants to communicate with you. It can speak your language.

1. What do you want to know about your visitor and the place he or she comes from?
2. What things will the visitor need to know in order to survive on your planet?
3. What would you like to tell this being about your planet and its people?

Exercise 10: Reading

Read the text that follows and answer the questions. Discuss your answers with a classmate.

The Pioneer 10 Space Probe

(1) The mission of the Pioneer 10 Space Probe came to an end in 1997 after the ship had been exploring space for nearly twenty-five years. Pioneer 10 was first launched by NASA in 1972 and sent on a twenty-one-month mission to explore the area around Jupiter. Many scientists did not believe that the small spaceship could survive the journey to Jupiter, but it did, and the mission was a great success.

(2) The Pioneer 10 mission was successful for three reasons. It sent us the first close-up photographs and measurements of the planet Jupiter. Scientists used this information to confirm that the giant planet is made up of gases and liquids. Then, as it traveled past Jupiter, Pioneer 10 became the first spaceship to use the gravity of a planet to push it along—a method that is now used routinely in space travel. And finally, the space probe showed that our solar system is much larger than scientists previously imagined. When the mission ended the ship was 6.2 billion miles away from Earth and had still not traveled outside of our solar system!

(3) Scientists had hoped to find the boundary between our solar system and

interstellar space. Unfortunately, after 25 years in space, Pioneer 10 has run low on power, and scientists are not able to use its instruments anymore. Even though its mission is formally over, scientists at the NASA Research Center in California will continue to listen to the soft "beeps" from the Pioneer 10 radio until its battery goes dead sometime in 1999.

(4)   After the radio stops, the ship will travel on to the star Aldebaran, which is about sixty-eight light years, or about two million years of travel, away. And the spaceship's unofficial mission will continue—if Sagan's gold-plated plaque showing images of a man and a woman, the path of the spaceship and our sun's location in the galaxy is still whole. As one scientist remarked, "If the plaque were ever found by other beings, it would be wonderful. But it's a big space out there, a big galaxy, a big universe."

Questions
1. What was the purpose of the Pioneer 10 mission? Was the mission successful? Why or why not?
2. What three things were accomplished by the Pioneer 10 mission? Which do you feel was the most important? Why?
3. Reread paragraph 3. If the prefix *inter* means *between or among* and *stellar* means *of a star or stars,* what do you think the word *interstellar* means?
4. Carl Sagan was interested in the "unofficial" mission of the Pioneer 10 spaceship. What was its unofficial mission?

Exercise 11: Writing

In the first reading, "A Love Affair with Science," Sagan makes two points.

1. It is important for ordinary people to know and understand science.
2. Modern TV and radio programs are a "kind of celebration of ignorance" that teaches that study and learning are things to avoid.

Do you agree or disagree with Sagan? Choose point 1 or 2 and explain your opinion about it in a short essay. Support your ideas with evidence or examples from your own life.

Writing for Different Discourse Communities

Think about writing in different situations and for different audiences. Do you write a letter to a friend using the same style and vocabulary as when you write a letter to a business associate? Generally, no. A letter to a friend is often very informal, uses conversational language, and does not need to follow special rules about form. A business letter, on the other hand, is more formal, uses vocabulary related to business, and does follow rules about form. A friend and a business associate are members of two different *discourse communities.* A discourse community is a group of people who share specific interests, goals, vocabulary, writing styles, and ways of sharing information or giving one another feedback. Another example of a discourse community would be your professors and teachers at the university. Can you think of different discourse communities within the university? Write their names here.

_____   _____   _____

In order to be successful in your studies you will need to learn and follow different *conventions,* or set ways of doing things, when writing for different discourse communities in the university.

It is also important to realize that writing conventions are different from culture to culture, even for the same discourse community. The standard format of a Japanese business letter is very different from the standard format of an American business letter. Likewise, the conventions of writing at universities in your country are probably quite different from the conventions you will need to follow at a school in the United States.

Exercise 12: Writing

Practice writing for two different discourse communities by producing the two following texts.

a. As part of your advanced ESL class this term, you are exchanging diary entries with an ESL student enrolled in a different astronomy class section from your own. These informal diary entries are the kind you would write to a friend telling him or her what happened in class during the week (the topics covered in class, what you learned, your comments and reactions, etc.). The topic in class this week was Carl Sagan, and one of the assigned readings was the text in this book. Based on what you learned about Sagan, write a two to three paragraph diary entry for this week.

b. Write a two to three paragraph essay in answer to the following test question.

What reasons does Carl Sagan give for wanting to popularize science?

Unit 9
Colin Powell

Vocabulary Preview

Preview 1

Complete each sentence with the most suitable word.

allied   commit   team   rigorous   reliable

1. In mid-April, after _____ Forces defeated Iraq, Powell returned to the South Bronx.
2. "We are all together in this," said the soldier. "We are all part of a _____."
3. According to him, American soldiers are motivated, self-confident, and _____.
4. "Our standards in our schools," said Powell, "must be high and _____."
5. Powell advised students to _____ totally to an education.

Preview 2

Look at the way the underlined words are used in the sentences. Match each word with its definition by writing the letter of the correct definition on the line.

1. Expert witnesses are expected to have specialized knowledge, skill or experience in the area of their testimony.
2. A playwright must be constantly aware of the audience in the writing, structure, and timing of a play.
3. Childless for a long time, Hannah prayed for a son, promising to dedicate him to God.
4. Pedigreed dogs are expected to conform to a set standard of appearance.

5. Managers face the <u>task</u> of supervising projects that are influenced by a number of factors.

___ 1. expert   a. attentive to
___ 2. aware   b. job
___ 3. dedicate   c. informed
___ 4. conform   d. correspond
___ 5. task   e. offer, give, consecrate

Reading Preview: What Do You Know about Colin Powell?

Circle the correct answer. If you don't know the answer, guess.

1. Colin Powell is
   a. an Asian American
   b. an African American
   c. a Native American
   d. a Mexican American

2. He has worked most of his professional life in
   a. government
   b. education
   c. the military
   d. business

3. He became
   a. a four-star general
   b. national security advisor
   c. chairman of the Joint Chiefs of Staff
   d. all of the above

From *Colin Powell: Soldier/Statesman - Statesman/Soldier* by Howard Means (New York: Penguin Putnam, 1992), 32–37 and 92–93.

Introduction to the Readings

Colin Powell is the embodiment of the American dream. He was born in **Harlem** to immigrant parents. He overcame the rough life of the streets to become a four-star general, national security advisor, and chairman of the Joint Chiefs of Staff. He was also the mastermind of Desert Storm, the military confrontation between Iraq and the United States in 1990–91.

The two excerpts that follow are from Howard Means's *Colin Powell: Soldier/Statesman - Statesman/Soldier.* The first excerpt, "We Are All Family," is part of a speech he delivered to students at the high school he had attended thirty years earlier. The second, "At **Tuskegee**," is part of an eloquent speech he gave at the national convention of the Tuskegee Airmen, the famous African American fighter pilots of World War II.

Reading 1: We Are All Family

(1)   In mid-April 1991, a month and a half after **Allied Forces** had expelled Saddam Hussein's army from **Kuwait**, Colin Powell returned to the South Bronx as one of the most celebrated military leaders of modern history, living proof of the dreams that **Izetta Skelton** and other **Hunts Point** parents harbor for their children. He began his visit with a tour of the last major defense contractor left in New York City, the Loral Corporation Defense Electronic Manufacturing Plant in the Bronx, where radar warning systems used by U.S. aircraft during Desert Storm had been produced. During the visit, Loral executives told Powell they were establishing a $6,000 annual scholarship in his name so that a graduate of his high school, Morris High, could attend his other alma mater, City College.

Harlem: a neighborhood of the Bronx, an area of New York City
Tuskegee: a famous institution of higher education for African Americans that trained fighter pilots during World War II
Allied Forces: the armed forces of all of the countries that joined together in fighting Saddam Hussein
Kuwait: A country in the Middle East attacked by the neighboring country of Iraq in 1991. The military confrontation, led in Iraq by Iraqi ruler Saddam Hussein, led to the Gulf War, also known as "Desert Storm."
Izetta Skelton: an immigrant living in Hunts Point
Hunts Point: The neighborhood where Powell grew up. Hunts Point is part of New York City.

(2)   From there Powell went to the fortresslike Morris High School at 166th Street and Boston Road, where he urged the students to stay in school. "If you don't get that school diploma," Powell told them, "you are on your way to nowhere. You are on your way to the dead end. In fact, if you don't get that high school diploma, you probably can't even get into my Army these days . . . Over ninety-seven percent of the **GIs** who are serving have their high school diploma." The reason the Army almost demands a diploma these days is simple, Powell went on. It's proof that the person who earned it is "somebody who will stick to the task given. Somebody who, growing in their life at age fourteen, fifteen, sixteen, seventeen, when faced with a challenge of hard work, of study, of commitment, of responsibility . . . met the challenge, stayed in high school, and got that diploma. It shows that you can overcome obstacles."

(3)   Powell's visit to the school was his first since he had graduated nearly thirty-seven years earlier. "I remember this place," he told the students. "I remember . . . the route I used to take each day from my home on Kelly Street to school. I also remember, upon occasion, experiencing the feeling 'you can't make it.' But you can. When I was coming up, opportunities were limited. But now the opportunities are there to be anything you want to be. But wanting to be isn't enough. Dreaming about it isn't enough. You've got to study for it, work for it, fight for it with all your heart, energy, and soul, so that nothing will be denied you."

(4)   The following evening, at Manhattan's Waldorf Astoria Hotel, in an address to the Association for a Better New York, Powell reflected on his visit, the beloved Army that had by then consumed thirty-three years of his life, and the lessons that could be taken from its performance in the Persian Gulf War. It was the sort of speech that makes political consultants weak in their knees when they think of the possibility—however faint—of someday having a candidate Powell to run. Were Powell ever to enter politics, it would be the very model of a stump speech, his short-course version of how to make America the place it once was, the place he seems fervently to believe it can be again.

GI: slang for "soldier"

(5)   During the war, Powell said, he had watched an episode of ABC-TV's **Prime Time Live** in which Sam Donaldson, on location in Saudi Arabia, interviewed some members of a tank company of the First Armored Division—part of the Army's VII Corps, which had just been flown in from Germany.

(6)   "First you see an Asian American soldier," Powell said. "Then there's a white American sergeant who says a few words, and then a black soldier—an Afro-American—and then another white soldier, and then an old grizzled black sergeant who says a few words, and finally another white soldier who says he's from Texas. He concludes the little piece by saying that he's honored to be an American and honored to be in the United States Army. But it's the first black soldier who said something that was so significant to me.

(7)   "He looked like he was about nineteen years old. His language wasn't perfect, but he was articulate. And he sat there, on a case of rations, and behind him you could see the other troops in his platoon standing there. You could see that they were white and they were black and that they were a family. Here's what the young soldier said: 'We've all been through the same training, and it instills confidence inside you and lets you know that no matter what it comes down to, you're around family. All of us are family. All these guys right here are my family.' And then you hear the grunts and shouts of his buddies. And you're familiar with what our troops today now say: 'Huu-ahh! Huu-ahh!' You've heard it on a thousand interviews. All of those teenagers, my kids, bonded together as a family, knowing that they were going to face danger, said: 'Huu-ahh.'

(8)   "The bond in that family of soldiers, tankers awash in the middle of a sea of sand, was so strong that they would die for each other. That's what makes a hero. They'll die for each other, and they'll die for their duty. And every year your Armed Forces creates that kind of bonding among about three hundred thousand young men and women who come in and who leave. Young whites will go back to their homes all over the country having been family with young blacks. And young blacks who go back to their homes all over this country having been treated as an equal brother with their white colleagues.

(9)   "Look at these youngsters for a moment. You've seen them all over television. They're a cross-section of America. Notwithstanding the pre-war pronouncements by so-called **demographic experts**, these young men and women come from all walks of American life. And they're clean, smart,

---

Prime Time Live: a news-oriented weekly TV show anchored by Sam Donaldson and Diane Sawyer
demographic experts: people with statistical knowledge of characteristics of different groups in a population

dedicated, trained, motivated, responsible, reliable, self-confident, selfless, patriotic, drug-free, respectful, tolerant, and caring."

(10)   Powell then went on to ask rhetorically if the experience of the Army is transferable to the civil sector. "You bet your life it is," he answered, "and the answer starts in school. It starts in schools such as Morris High School . . . and at thousands of other such schools across America. In our schools, we must have high expectations for our children—parents and teachers must have them. We must want our children to learn. We must want our children to succeed.

(11)   "In our schools, we must have discipline and we must have high standards. To enforce that discipline and those high standards we must have a working system of rewards and punishments–a working system, not a paper system, and not a system simply to satisfy a bureaucracy. In our schools, what we teach our children must be meaningful; it must conform to the high standards we've set up; and our evaluation of their progress through these standards must be rigorous and demanding.

(12)   "In our schools, we must teach our children that alone it is difficult to accomplish things but that together, as a team, as a family, almost anything can be accomplished. The challenges are there to be overcome and not to become a burden to press you into the ground. And in our schools, we need to motivate our children, motivate them to be responsible and accountable for their actions. Eventually, they'll learn to motivate themselves.

(13)   "I know schools can't be run like an infantry platoon," he concluded, "but it seems to me it was kind of like one when I went to school. But if we can work toward the standards I've just tried to describe to you briefly, I believe America will be well on the way to the twenty-first century full of hope, full of promise and a renewed sense of what matters in life. Like the young black soldier in the desert, we would come to know that we can all depend on one another; we could come to know that 'all of us are family.'"

Reading 2: At Tuskegee

Tuskegee Airmen. Photo compliments of Tuskegee University Archives. Reprinted with permission.

(14)   That Colin Powell is acutely aware of the segregated past of the Army that has been his home for more than thirty years, that he feels a debt to the black men and women who served in those armed forces, was never more evident than in August of 1991 when he addressed the twentieth annual national convention of the Tuskegee Airmen in Detroit.

(15)   "At Tuskegee, surrounded by some of the most vicious racism in America, the best and the brightest of their time set their individual and collective minds to what, even in retrospect, seemed an incredibly impossible task," Powell told the surviving airmen and their guests. "The men—and women— at Tuskegee didn't just need to master aviation and military skills and the support of their husbands in time of war. They had to do it while much of the power of the United States Army tried to sabotage the entire enterprise. While the civilians who surrounded them wasted no opportunity to express their hatred. While some of the very people who were teaching them their new

aviation skills believed without question in their ultimate failure. And while the general feelings of the people in America were at best those of neglect and at worst violent disagreement with the whole idea.

(16)   "But these were not ordinary men and women at Tuskegee," Powell went on. "If there is one thing about the history of the Tuskegee Airmen that is as unmistakable as the **silhouette** of a **P-51**, it is the fact that *these were not ordinary people* [Powell's emphasis]. They were *extraordinary* men and women. Like **Jackie Robinson**, they stood above the crowd. They brooked no opposition to their goals, accepted no shortcuts, and took solace in the fact that they were paving the way to the future. Courage. Character. Determination. Drive. Devotion to duty. Love of America despite her imperfections. These are the things that made up their character, that gave it strength, that gave it resilience, and pointed the way to the future.

(17)   "It is on this road to the future, paved with the sacrifice and blood of black patriots—especially the Tuskegee Airmen–it was on this road that I traveled to become the first black chairman of the Joint Chiefs of Staff. I never forget for a day, or for an hour, or for a minute, that I climbed to my position on the backs of the courageous African American men and women who went before me."

Comprehension Check

Check your understanding of the reading selections by marking these sentences true (*T*) or false (*F*).

___ 1. Colin Powell migrated to the United States at an early age.

___ 2. He grew up in Harlem, a neighborhood in the Bronx.

___ 3. Powell's main plea to students at Richard Morris High School was to join the military.

___ 4. According to Powell, most soldiers in the military come to feel that they are all one family.

___ 5. Powell makes a point about the military being all one family by telling a story about a military unit in Vietnam.

silhouette: outline, shape, image
P-51: a type of airplane
Jackie Robinson: The first African American to be allowed to play professional baseball in the major leagues.

___ 6. The Tuskegee Airmen were a unit of African American fighter
pilots who distinguished themselves during Desert Storm.

___ 7. Powell's message to the surviving Tuskegee Airmen underscores
how much he has been able to do for African Americans in his
role as chairman of the Joint Chiefs of Staff

___ 8. According to the reading, Powell makes the kind of speeches that
would make him an excellent political candidate.

Word Study

 University Word List Vocabulary .

allied	dedicate	military
aware	devote	reliable
challenge	eloquent	rigorous
commitment	expert	task
conform	goal	team

Understanding Words

Word Parts

Exercise 1: Prefixes

The prefix *con-*, as in *conform*, means *totally*, *together*, or *with*. Use one of the words starting with *con-* to complete each sentence.

consensus	convene	contact	contract
confrontation	congregation	conform	consult

1. The _____ between the rioters and the police was horrible! Several people were seriously hurt.

2. The rental _____ said that the tenant was responsible for paying all utilities, as well as $750 rent, every month.

3. The meeting was _____ in the conference room; his office couldn't handle ten people.

4. St. Mark's church has a very active _____; the members are always having one activity after another.

5. The _____ was that he did not deserve an Olympic medal.

6. Her new plan did not _____ to her parents' wishes; she wanted to study in France, they wanted her to stay home.

7. You can't _____ him until this evening; he'll be in New York until seven.

8. A psychologist was _____ to see what could be done about the boy's inferiority complex.

Exercise 2: Word Parts

Think about the word *unreliable*.

1. What is its root?   _____

2. What does its root mean?   _____

3. What is its prefix?   _____

4. What does the prefix mean?   _____

5. What is its suffix?   _____

6. What does it mean?   _____

7. What are some synonyms for *reliable?*   _____

8. What are some antonyms of *reliable?*   _____

9. An *unreliable* person is someone who   _____

Exercise 3: Word Parts

Think about the word *challenger*.

1. What is its root?   _____

2. What does its root mean?   _____

3. What is its suffix?   _____

4. What does the suffix mean?   _____

5. What are some synonyms for
   challenger?   _____

6. What are some antonyms of
   challenger?   _____

7. A *challenger* is someone who   _____

Word Relationships

Exercise 4: Synonyms

Cross out the word in each series that is not a synonym for the first
word in that series. Use your dictionary if necessary.

1. team	squad	crew	person	platoon
2. aware	alert	conscious	informed	ignorant
3. task	assignment	job	luxury	responsibility
4. goal	objective	hope	aim	intention
5. conform	rebel	obey	follow	agree
6. expert	specialist	amateur	authority	master
7. eloquent	expressive	unclear	fluent	articulate
8. rigorous	careless	exact	demanding	strict

Exercise 5: Collocations

Match items 1 through 5 with their common collocations by writing the
combinations on the lines following items 1 through 5.

Nouns

speaker	spirit	speech
weapons	operations	appeal
force	leader	gesture
forces		

1. eloquent

   _____

   _____

2. team

_____

_____

3. allied

_____

_____

4. task

_____

_____

5. military

_____

_____

The Grammar of Words

Exercise 6

Complete each sentence with the appropriate word form.

1. The parts were expertly _____ by the operator.
   assembled   assembly   assembler   assembling

2. We should not _____ on anyone but ourselves.
   reliance   reliable   rely   relying

3. _____ issues are not often fully understood by civilians.
   militant   militarized   militia   military

4. The nuns were at their _____ all day praying for the
   hostages.
   devotions   devoted   devotional   devote

5. The park was _____ to the memory of John F. Kennedy.
   dedication   dedicate   dedicated   dedicating

6. The Peace Corps was totally _____ to helping undeveloped
   countries.
   commit   committing   committed   commitment

Word Meanings

Exercise 7: Semantic Mapping

In this word map (semantic map) of military terms, write in each word or term under the appropriate subcategory.

sergeant	platoon	chairman of the Joint Chiefs of Staff
Gulf War	P-51	First Armored Division
tankers	GI	military leaders
aircraft	Desert Storm	defense contractor
airmen	VII Corps	
general	tank company	

Military Terms

People	Event	Equipment	Rank	Organizational Unit
_____	_____	_____	_____	_____
_____	_____	_____	_____	_____
_____	_____	_____	_____	_____
_____	_____	_____	_____	_____
_____	_____	_____	_____	_____
_____	_____	_____	_____	_____

Understanding Words in Sentences

Word Meanings in Context

Exercise 8

In the reading passages, scan for the words and phrase given in the following list. The number of the paragraph containing the word or phrase is given in parentheses. Circle the letter of the meaning that is most appropriate within the context of the reading passage.

1. allied (1)
   a. connected by treaty
   b. in close association
   c. connected by family

2. consumed (4)
   a. used up
   b. altered
   c. destroyed

3. episode (5)
   a. circumstance
   b. incident
   c. chapter

4. significant (6)
   a. vital
   b. meaningful
   c. influential

5. experts (9)
   a. knowledgeable people
   b. people in authority
   c. mathematicians

6. transferable (10)
   a. can be delivered
   b. can be transported
   c. can be shifted

7. accomplish (12)
   a. finish
   b. achieve
   c. perform

8. aware of (14)
   a. know about
   b. suspect
   c. want

Exercise 9

Reread the following passages from the text. Then complete the sentences or answer the questions by circling the letter of the correct choice.

1. The reason the Army almost demands a diploma these days is simple, Powell went on. It's proof that the person who earned it is "somebody who will stick to the task given. Somebody who, growing in their life at age fourteen, fifteen, sixteen, seventeen, when faced with a challenge of hard work, of study, of commitment, of responsibility . . . met the challenge, stayed in high school, and got that diploma. It shows that you can overcome obstacles."

   According to Powell, what was the greatest challenge Morris High School students faced?
   a. keeping safe in a tough neighborhood
   b. staying in school
   c. finishing their military training

2. "I remember . . . the route I used to take each day from my home on Kelly Street to school. I also remember, upon occasion, experiencing the feeling 'you can't make it.' But you can. When I was coming up, opportunities were limited. But now the opportunities are there to be anything you want to be. "

   At times, what feelings did Powell have about his future?
   a. that he might not be able to succeed
   b. that he could be anything he wanted to be
   c. that he needed to leave his country in order to fulfill his dreams

3. "He looked like he was about nineteen years old. His language wasn't perfect, but he was articulate. And he sat there, on a case of rations, and behind him you could see the other troops in his platoon standing there. You could see that they were white and they were black and that they were a family. Here's what the young soldier said: 'We've all been through the same training, and it instills confidence inside you and lets you know that no matter what it comes down to, you're around family.'"

   In the Army, the soldier felt
   a. that he was all alone in the world
   b. that he had lost his confidence
   c. that he was not alone

4. "If there is one thing about the history of the Tuskegee Airmen that is as unmistakable as the silhouette of a P-51, it is the fact that *these were not ordinary people* [Powell's emphasis]. They were *extraordinary* men and women. Like Jackie Robinson, they stood above the crowd. They brooked no opposition to their goals, accepted no shortcuts, and took solace in the fact that they were paving the way to the future. Courage. Character. Determination. Drive. Devotion to duty. Love of America despite her imperfections."

   At Tuskegee, the airmen felt
   a. that they would have to compromise to achieve their goals
   b. that their country was full of imperfections
   c. that, eventually, they would make their dreams come true

5. "It is on this road to the future, paved with the sacrifice and blood of black patriots—especially the Tuskegee Airmen—it was on this road that I traveled to become the first black chairman of the Joint Chiefs of Staff. I never forget for a day, or for an hour, or for a minute, that I climbed to my position on the backs of the courageous African American men and women who went before me. "

Powell gave credit for his success
a. to the black men and women who had preceded him
b. to his school
c. to the Army

Using Words in Communication

Exercise 10: Speaking

Working in pairs, discuss the following questions.

1. What is the American dream? Why has Colin Powell been called the embodiment of the American dream?
2. According to Powell, why is finishing high school a good indicator of a person's character?
3. What values held by the military does Powell regard as transferable to civilian life, particularly to educating young people?
4. Why does Powell regard the Tuskegee Airmen as extraordinary?
5. What are Colin Powell's feelings about his country?

Exercise 11: Speaking

Study the following questions for a few moments. Think of how you might answer them. Then take turns asking and answering the questions with another student.

1. Has your country been involved in a war?
2. Why was the war fought?
3. How could the conflict have been resolved without resorting to war?
4. How did the people in your country feel about the war?
5. How did the war end?
6. Who were the military leaders?
7. Were there any heroes?

Exercise 12: Reading

Use the following words to complete this reading selection.

aware	dedicated	military
challenge	devoted	relied
conform	eloquent	task

Plato's Ideal Society

Preeminent among the Greeks of the fifth century B.C. was Plato, the Athenian philosopher who is best remembered today for *The Republic,* the dialogue in which he presents an _____ vision of the ideal society. *The Republic* is primarily _____ to Plato's notion that only the wise should rule. Plato was against the idea that men should rule just because they had proven to be powerful _____ leaders. All one had to do, Plato pointed out, was to look at what Pericles, a renowned general and statesman of Athens, had done for his people. True, he had _____ much of his energy to the beautification of Athens, but he had also plunged his beloved city-state into a disastrous war that had ultimately led to its downfall.

The _____ facing every man, Plato argued, was to search for eternal wisdom. Only those who dedicated many years of their lives to considering eternal questions such as, What is truth? What is honor? What is justice? ultimately arrived at wisdom and were then qualified to become philosopher-kings.

Many people are not _____ of the fact that Plato was one of our first feminists. Unlike almost every other well-known thinker of his time, Plato held that women could become as wise as men and thus could also be

_____ upon to provide wise guardianship.

But what about the rest of the people; what was their role to be in Plato's ideal society? Well, those who were spirited, courageous, and interested in honor and glory were to become the protectors and defenders of the state.

The rest, the common people, were to be laborers whose _____ it would be to employ whatever special gift or ability they had for the benefit of the state.

And what if some of these common people refused to _____ to what the state dictated for them? Well, said Plato, they would have to be taught the value of working for the common good.

Exercise 13: Writing

Practice writing for two different discourse communities by producing the two following texts.

a. Write a three to five paragraph letter to the editor of the *Washington Post* supporting *or* protesting the 1998 U.S. bombing of terrorist training camps in Afghanistan and of a Sudanese pharmaceutical company in retaliation for the bombing of the American embassies in Africa.
b. Write an informal letter to your Sudanese friend in Sudan with your comments and reactions to the bombing.

Review Unit 3

I. Choose the correct word from the list on the left to go with each meaning. (In each set, you will not use two of the words.)

Set A

1. allied
2. concentrate
3. controversial
4. fertile
5. arbitrary

— causing strong differing opinions
— rich, productive
— to focus

Set B

1. attain
2. challenge
3. reveal
4. interpret
5. consume

— to use something up
— a test, a difficult task
— to show or uncover

Set C

1. task
2. element
3. principle
4. diameter
5. statistic

— basic idea or concept
— information expressed in numbers
— a part or quality

II. Cross out the word in each series that is not a synonym for the first word in that series.

1. construct   create   build   repair
2. commitment   promise   lie   obligation
3. sociology   psychology   geology   anthropology
4. part   component   element   method
5. enrich   finance   improve   supplement

III. Match each word on the left with its antonym by writing the letter of the correct antonym on the line.

— 1. expert	a. inferior
— 2. contract	b. quit
— 3. superior	c. amateur
— 4. complex	d. reliable
— 5. persist	e. expand
	f. simple

IV. Match these prefixes and suffixes with the correct words to make the words that are defined. Write out each complete word in the space provided.

mis-   trans-   -ity   -or   non-   -ology

_____ 1. _____ + violent = peaceful
_____ 2. bio + _____ = the study of living things
_____ 3. _____ + understand = to understand incorrectly
_____ 4. _____ + form = to change from one state to
                another
_____ 5. fertile + _____ = the state of being fertile,
                productive
_____ 6. create + _____ = a person who creates
                something

V. Match each word on the left with a common collocation by writing the letter of the correct choice on the line.

— 1. military	a. art
— 2. team	b. shock
— 3. visual	c. behavior
— 4. culture	d. ally
— 5. scientific	e. player
— 6. assembly	f. mental
— 7. appropriate	g. theory
	h. line

VI. Complete each sentence with one of the words given here. You may need to change the form of the word or add word endings.

solar	evident	illustrate	intellect
eloquent	generate	option	exponent

1. The _____ of the nude man and woman on the Pioneer 10 plaque shocked only a few people.

2. The Vietnam War Memorial initially _____ a lot of controversy, but now it is one of the most visited monuments in Washington, D.C.

3. Maya didn't have the _____ of having a private room because the hotel was too full.

4. Car manufacturers hope to one day develop a car that runs on

   _____ energy.

5. Dr. Martin Luther King, Jr., was one of the most _____ speakers of the civil rights movement.

University Word List Index

This list, compiled by Xue and Nation (1984), contains approximately 800 words that students need to know in order to read college-level texts. Words studied in this text are set in bold-faced type and marked by the number of the unit and page number on which they appear.

A
abandon
abnormal
absorb
abstract (abstraction) (7:127)
academic
accelerate
access
accompany
accomplish (3:41)
accumulate
accurate
achieve
acid
acquire
adapt (1:7)
adequate
adhere
adjacent
adjective
adjust **(adjustments)** (2:26)
administer
adolescent
adult
advocate
aesthetic
affiliate
affluence
aggregate

aggression
agitate
aid
alcohol (6:106)
align
allege
allocate
allude
ally **(allied)** (9:164)
alter
alternative
ambiguity
amorphous
analogy
analyze
angular
annual
anomaly
anonymous
anthropology
apparatus
appeal
append
appendix
appraise
appreciate
approach (3:44)
appropriate (2:24)
approximate

arbitrary (4:66)
area
aristocrat
arithmetic
arouse
ascribe
aspect
aspiration
assemble **(assembly)** (1:7)
assent
assert
assess
asset
assign (4:66)
assimilate
assist (5:88)
assume
assure
astronomy
atmosphere
atom
attach
attain (5:86)
attitude
attribute
auspices
authorize
automatic (1:7)
avail **(available)** (1:7)

G. Xue and I. S. P. Nation, "A university word list," *Language Learning and Communication* 3 (1984): 215–29.

averse
aware (9:168)
awe
axis

B
battery
benefit
biology
bomb
bore
breed
bubble
bulk
bureaucracy

C
calendar
cancel
capable
capture
carbon
career (6:105)
catalog
category
cater
cease
cell
challenge (9:165)
channel
chapter
chemical
circuit
circulate
circumstance
civic
clarify
classic
client
clinic
code
coefficient
cogent
coincide
collapse
collide
colloquial
column
comment

commit **(commitment)**
 (9:165)
commodity
commune **(community)**
 (5:86)
communicate (8:147)
compel
compensate
competence
complement
complex (3:41)
complicate (2:25)
comply
component (1:7)
compound
comprehend (4:68)
comprise
compulsion
compute
conceive (4:70)
concentrate (6:104)
concentric
concept (4:70)
conclude
condense
conduct (3:41)
confer
configuration
confine
conflict
conform (9:167)
confront
congress
conjunction
consent
consequent
conserve
consist
console
constant
constitute
construct (8:147)
construe
consult (6:105)
consume **(consumer)** (1:5)
contact (8:147)
contaminate
contemplate
contend

context
continent
contingent
contract (4:65)
contradict
contrary
contrast
contribute
controversy **(controversial)**
 (8:148)
convene
converge
converse
convert
cooperate
coordinate
corporate
correlate
correspond
create (4:70)
credible
creditor
crisis
criterion
critic (7:128)
crucial (5:88)
crystal
culture (4:69)
cumbersome
currency
cycle
cylinder

D
data
debate
decade (1:5)
decimal
decline
dedicate (9:167)
defect
defer
deficient
define
definite
deflect
degenerate
degrade
deliberate

Answer Key

Unit 1: Lee Iacocca

Vocabulary Preview

Preview 1 (p. 2)
1. economy
2. consumers
3. research
4. features
5. options

Preview 2 (p. 2)
1. c
2. d
3. e
4. a
5. b

Reading Preview (p. 3)
1. c
2. b
3. a

Comprehension Check (p. 8)
1. F
2. T
3. F
4. T
5. F
6. T
7. F
8. F
9. T
10. T

Exercise 1 (p. 9)
1. c
2. e
3. b
4. a
5. d

Exercise 2 (p. 10)
1. c
2. d
3. h
4. b
5. a
6. e
7. f
8. g

Exercise 3 (p. 10)
1. a car designer
2. an economist
3. a market researcher
4. an accountant
5. an entertainer

Exercise 4 (p. 11)
1. S
2. A
3. A
4. S
5. S
6. S
7. S
8. A

Exercise 5 (p. 12)
Answers will vary but might include
Economy cars: Volkswagen, Honda
Civic, Toyota
Luxury cars: Cadillac, BMW,
Mercedes, Rolls Royce

Exercise 6 (p. 12)
1. e
2. a
3. d
4. b
5. c

Exercise 7 (p. 13)
1. economically
2. economical
3. economy
4. economize
5. Economics
6. economist

Exercise 8 (p. 15)
1. b
2. a
3. c
4. e
5. d

Exercise 9 (p. 15)
1. b
2. b
3. b
4. c
5. c
6. c
7. b
8. a

Exercise 10 (p. 16)
1. consuming
2. researched
3. available
4. huge
5. function
6. automatic

Exercise 13 (p. 18)
Answers will vary. Sample essay:
Two important factors led to the success of the Mustang in the early 1960s. In the first place, the economy was thriving. The end of the war in 1945 had brought about a period of great prosperity in the country, and Americans had more money than ever before to spend on cars.

Second, the market for cars was changing. Market research suggested that car buyers were different in this decade. There were increasing numbers of baby boomers ready to leave the city, move out to the suburbs, and start families. There was also a different kind of older car buyer.

Whereas for the past decade, more mature customers had shown interest only in durable, long-lasting cars like the Falcon, now, in the new optimistic, prosperous sixties, they were looking for something sportier and more luxurious. Also, there was a new kind of buyer, one never seen in such great numbers—single women. During the war large numbers of single women had acquired sophisticated skills that enabled them not just to work as teachers and secretaries but as highly paid employees in all fields. These liberated single women were looking for a car that would reflect their independent spirit. They wanted a car with great style and performance.

It was an ideal time for the design and development of a stylish, luxurious, sporty car. It was an ideal time for the Mustang.

Unit 2: Maya Lin

Vocabulary Preview

Preview 1 (p. 20)
1. site
2. quote
3. appropriate
4. complicated
5. adjustments

Preview 2 (p. 20)
1. a
2. e
3. d
4. b
5. c

Reading Preview (p. 21)
1. a
2. b
3. a

Comprehension Check (p. 26)
1. T
2. F
3. T
4. F

5. T
6. F
7. T
8. F

Exercise 1 (p. 28)
1. b
2. b
3. b
4. a
5. c

Exercise 2 (p. 29)
1. prohibited
2. specify
3. lowest
4. unsuitable
5. simple
6. position

Exercise 3 (p. 29)
1. d
2. e
3. f
4. a
5. b
6. c

Exercise 4 (p. 30)
1. appropriate
2. psychology
3. optional
4. luxury
5. researcher
6. consumer
7. impression
8. decade

Exercise 5 (p. 31)
1. impressionable
2. impress
3. impressive
4. impression
5. impression

Exercise 6 (p. 31)
1. d
2. a
3. c
4. b

Exercise 7 (p. 32)
Answers will vary but might include the following.

| | | | | Formal |
House	Beach	School	Work	Dance
robe	bathing	jeans	business	long
shorts	suit	dress	suit	dress
slippers	sandals	boots	skirt	tuxedo
jeans	shorts	sweater	sweater	
sweat	jeans	skirt	jumper	
pants		uniform		
sweater		jumper		
skirt				
jumper				

Exercise 8 (p. 32)
legal aid, legal matters, legal age, legal holiday, legal issues, legal rights
psychological tests, psychological evaluation
minimum wage, minimum speed, minimum age, minimum income
adjusted wage, adjusted income

Exercise 9 (p. 33)
1. c
2. b
3. c
4. b
5. a
6. c

Exercise 10 (p. 35)
Possible answers:
historical significance, civil rights movement, memorial, movement, marches, landmark legal decisions, Martin Luther King, Jr., assassinated, monuments, people connected with the civil rights movement, era, a people's movement, given their lives

Exercise 13 (p. 36)
1. Maya Lin
2. Martin Luther King, Jr.
3. one little girl
4. Morris Dees

Unit 3: Roberto Clemente

Vocabulary Preview

Preview 1 (p. 39)
1. terror
2. evident
3. statistics
4. supplemented
5. withdrawn

Preview 2 (p. 39)
1. d
2. c
3. a
4. e
5. b

Reading Preview (p. 40)
1. b
2. a
3. a

Comprehension Check (p. 45)
1. T
2. F
3. T
4. T
5. T
6. F
7. T
8. F

Exercise 1 (p. 47)
1. legislature
2. illegal
3. legislator
4. Illegitimate
5. legal
6. legislate

Exercise 2 (p. 48)

in-	mis-	un-
inappropriate	misquote	unattainable
involuntary	misconduct	uncomplicated
	misappropriate	unemotional
		unavailable

1. unavailable
2. misconduct
3. inappropriate
4. uncomplicated
5. misquoting

6. unemotional

Exercise 3 (p. 49)
1. abandon
2. loser
3. guide
4. hear
5. concern
6. indifference

Exercise 4 (p. 49)
1. terrorism
2. terrorists
3. terrified
4. terrifying, terrible
5. terrorized, terrified

Exercise 5 (p. 50)
1. C
2. I
3. I
4. C
5. C
6. I

Exercise 6 (p. 51)
1. b
2. c
3. c
4. a
5. b
6. a

Exercise 7 (p. 51)
1. the feeling that you are better than or superior to everyone else
2. the feeling that you are not as good as everyone else
3. the feeling that everyone is out to get you
4. the feeling that you are responsible for something bad that has happened to someone else

Exercise 8 (p. 52)
1. In Greek legend, Oedipus was a king who, without knowing it, killed his father and married his mother.
2. The term *Oedipus complex* means the sexual feelings that a son has toward his mother.

Exercise 9 (p. 52)
1. b
2. e
3. a
4. d
5. c

Exercise 10 (p. 53)
1. a
2. a
3. c
4. a

Exercise 11 (p. 54)
1. a. a small frog
   b. an embrace
   c. a straw hat
2. In the text the definition followed the word.
3. see if a definition of the word appears in the text

Exercise 12 (p. 55)
1. c
2. a
3. b
4. b
5. a
6. c

Exercise 13 (p. 56)
Paragraph:

Unfortunately, soon after <u>taking off,</u> the <u>plane</u> developed <u>engine trouble.</u> A man living near the beach saw the plane <u>flying low</u> as it turned back to the airport. "Suddenly the <u>motors</u> <u>appeared to sputter</u> and <u>go dead,</u> " he said. "My wife said to me 'That plane is going to <u>crash.</u>'" Soon after, he heard <u>a loud noise.</u> He ran to the beach and saw the <u>plane floating on</u> <u>top of the water.</u> A few moments later he saw <u>it plunge into the ocean.</u> <u>Although a long search was</u> <u>conducted,</u> no survivors were ever <u>found.</u>

Exercise 14 (p. 56)
1. Clemente played in the World Series in 1960 and 1971.

2. Clemente played for the Pittsburgh Pirates.
3. Both years, he was at bat 29 times.
4. Clemente batted no home runs in the 1960 Series but he batted two in the 1971 Series.
5. Clemente's batting average in 1960 was good. He had 9 hits in that Series for a batting average of .310. His average in 1971, however, was much better. He had 12 hits, 2 doubles, 1 triple, and 2 home runs for a batting average of .414.

Exercise 15 (p. 57)
Answers will vary, but might include
a. surprised, homesick, puzzled, frustrated, offended, lonely, unhappy, hurt, confused
b. worried, anxious, energized, sympathetic, motivated
c. proud, happy, moved, excited, teary-eyed, touched

Review Unit 1

I. (p. 59)
A. 4, 1, 5
B. 2, 5, 3
C. 4, 1, 5

II. (p. 60)
1. S
2. A
3. S
4. S
5. S
6. S
7. A
8. S

III. (p. 60)
1. d
2. e
3. b
4. f
5. a
6. c
7. h
8. g

IV. (p. 60)
1. P
2. P
3. R
4. S
5. S
6. P
7. R
8. P
9. R
10. R, S

V. (p. 60)
Clues: definition, example, contrast, inference, direct explanation

VI. (p. 61)
1. d
2. e
3. b
4. c
5. a

VII. (p. 61)
1. features
2. conducted
3. approached
4. uttered
5. complex
6. adjusted
7. assembled
8. heroic

Unit 4: Maya Angelou

Vocabulary Preview

Preview 1 (p. 63)
1. layer
2. assigned
3. comprehend
4. cultures
5. residing

Preview 2 (p. 63)
1. b
2. d
3. a
4. e
5. c

Reading Preview (p. 64)
1. c

2. c
3. b

Comprehension Check (p. 70)
1. T
2. F
3. F
4. F
5. F
6. T
7. T
8. F
9. T
10. F

Exercise 1 (p. 71)
1. c
2. e
3. a
4. b
5. d

Exercise 2 (p. 72)
administrator, creator, demonstrator, conductor
1. conductor
2. creator
3. administrator
4. Demonstrators
some other words adding -or:
illustrator, editor, translator, counselor, legislator

Exercise 3 (p. 72)
1. employment contract
2. marriage contract
3. rental contract
4. business contract
common idea: c. a legal agreement to do something

Exercise 4 (p. 73)
1. name
2. activity
3. opinion
4. orchestra
5. sense
6. omit
7. resident
8. alternate

9. hope

10. idea

Exercise 5 (p. 74)

1. A, refers to a business agreement between two or more persons
2. B, refers to a thing becoming smaller or shorter
3. B, refers to shortening a word by omitting sounds or letters
4. C, refers to a disease
5. A, refers to a business arrangement for the supply of goods and services at a fixed price

Exercise 6 (p. 75)

1. b
2. c
3. c
4. a
5. c
6. b

Exercise 7 (p. 75)

1. create problems, create a work of art, create a text, create a situation, create a role
2. assign problems (as in homework), assign homework, assign a job to someone, assign a text, assign a role
3. comprehend a situation, comprehend what someone says, comprehend a work of art, comprehend homework, comprehend a text, comprehend a role (on stage)
4. contract tuberculosis, contract when cold, a marriage contract

Exercise 8 (p. 76)

1. overlapping
2. contracting and releasing, muscles
3. assigned arbitrarily
4. demonstrate his love, in revolt, layers of paper

Exercise 9 (p. 77)

Answers will vary.

Exercise 10 (p. 78)

Answers will vary.

Exercise 11 (p. 78)

Answers will vary.

Unit 5: Cesar Chavez

Vocabulary Preview

Preview 1 (p. 80)

1. primitive
2. goal
3. attain
4. sociologists
5. issues

Preview 2 (p. 80)

1. d
2. a
3. e
4. b
5. c

Reading Preview (p. 81)

1. d
2. a
3. a

Comprehension Check (p. 88)

1. F
2. T
3. T
4. F
5. F
6. T
7. T
8. T

Exercise 1 (p. 90)

1. crucial
2. persist
3. voluntary
4. exponents
5. eliminate
6. undertake

Exercise 2 (p. 91)

1. c
2. a
3. b
4. d
5. e
6. f

Exercise 3 (p. 91)
1. e
2. c
3. b
4. a
5. g
6. d
7. f

Exercise 4 (p. 92)
1. medical assistant: d, g
2. dental assistant: a, h
3. administrative assistant: c, e
4. legal assistant: b, f

Exercise 5 (p. 93)

Noun	Noun (person)	Adjective	Verb
assistance	*assistant*	assisted	assist
attainment	—	attainable	attain
persistence	—	persistent	*persist*
—	*volunteer*	voluntary	volunteer
elimination	eliminator	eliminated	eliminate
issue	issuer	issued	*issue*

Exercise 6 (p. 93)
1. C
2. I
3. C
4. I
5. C
6. C

Exercise 7 (p. 94)

Urban Centers	Suburbs
museums	swimming pools
office buildings	vegetable gardens
parking lots	trees and flowers

Exercise 8 (p. 94)
Answers will vary but could include
1. A psychologist is someone who attempts to find out how the client's mind works.
2. An economist is someone who knows a lot about the production and consumption or use of goods and services.
3. Impressionists were nineteenth-century painters who painted their general impression of a subject, without using a lot of details.
4. An archaeologist is someone who studies a culture by finding and studying its remains.

Exercise 9 (p. 94)

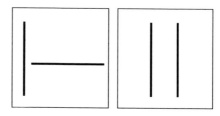

Exercise 10 (p. 95)
1. a
2. d
3. b
4. a
5. b

Exercise 11 (p. 96)
volunteered, dedicate evenings and weekends, voter registration drive, canvassed the area, knocking at every door, talked with people, told the people how they could effect change, voting for leaders who would help, made people see how important it was to vote, walked the streets, encouraging people to register, dedication paid off, general election, registered new voters

Exercise 12 (p. 97)
1. Who was the most famous exponent of passive resistance?
2. In the end, was his persistence rewarded?
3. What were migrant worker camps like?
4. Where did Ross establish his first CSO?
5. According to Ross, how could issues best be attacked?

Exercise 13 (p. 97)
Answers will vary.

Exercise 14 (p. 98)
Answers will vary.

Unit 6: Gloria Steinem

Vocabulary Preview

Preview 1 (p. 100)
1. transformation
2. consulted
3. income
4. mental
5. concentrate

Preview 2 (p. 100)
1. b
2. c
3. e
4. d
5. a

Reading Preview (p. 101)

1. b
2. a
3. c
4. a

Comprehension Check (p. 109)

1. T
2. F
3. T
4. T
5. F
6. F
7. T
8. F
9. T
10. T

Exercise 1 (p. 111)
1. translators
2. transporting
3. transmitted
4. transformation

Exercise 2 (p. 112)
1. concentrate—dilute
2. depressed—elated
3. income—expense
4. tiny—huge
5. reverse—forward
6. minimum—maximum

7. contract—expand
8. consume—produce
9. luxury—economy

Exercise 3 (p. 113)
1. alcohol : drug :: bread : food
   relationship: a specific item of a
   general category
2. nervous : calm :: tense : relaxed
   relationship: antonyms or words
   with opposite meanings
   or nervous : tense :: calm : relaxed
   relationship: If you are nervous you
   feel tense; if you are calm you feel
   relaxed.
3. advise : tell :: consult : ask
   relationship: When you advise you
   tell; when you consult you ask.
4. author : write :: editor : edit
   relationship: An author writes, and
   an editor edits.

Exercise 4 (p. 114)

Health	*Money*	*Emotions*	*Change*
alcohol	finance	nervous	evolve
consult	income	depressed	reverse
drug	economy	mental	transform
mental			

Other words will vary, but might
include
| doctor | bank | happy | alter |

Exercise 5 (p. 114)
1. b
2. c
3. a
4. b

Exercise 6 (p. 116)
1. c
2. b
3. a

Exercise 7 (p. 116)
Answers will vary, but could include
1. Ruth as a normal young person:
   energetic, loved basketball and
   reading, drove a car, was good at
   gardening, wore overalls, a good
   student, good at math and poetry,

part-time bookkeeper, rebellious,
fell in love
2. Ruth when she is mentally ill:
stayed in bed, heard voices, loving,
intelligent, terrorized, saw visions,
hard to understand her speech,
physically awkward, afraid to go
outside, frightened

Exercise 8 (p. 117)
Individual answers will vary.
1. Generally women were expected to
stay at home and take care of their
children. Husbands and children
were more important than a
woman's career.
2. Answers will vary.
3. Generally, most young men and
women expect to have more
freedom than their parents did in
choosing their own jobs and
lifestyles.

Exercise 9 (p. 117)
About twenty-three million people
in the United States have mental
conditions called "anxiety disorders."
One type of anxiety disorder is called
"agoraphobia." The term *agoraphobia*
comes from the Greek words *agora,*
meaning *marketplace,* and *phobia,*
meaning *a fear of something.* When a
person has agoraphobia he or she feels
very nervous and afraid when out in
open public places or in crowds of
people. Some people may actually feel
so nervous that they completely stop
going out and remain at home all the
time. When they do go out, people
with agoraphobia often experience
"panic attacks." During a panic attack
their bodies react as if they were in
extreme danger: their hearts beat very
fast, they sweat, and they feel knots in
their stomachs and lumps in their
throats.
Today there are two types of
treatment for these anxiety disorders.
The first is cognitive therapy. During
cognitive therapy the person learns

how to accept his or her fear and
function in spite of it. The person may
also learn relaxation and breathing
techniques or have some type of
"talking" therapy with a counselor.
The second type of treatment is
medication. A person's tendency
toward panic attacks and the severity
of his or her symptoms may be
affected by levels of certain chemicals
in his or her brain. There are many
drugs that can be used to help these
conditions. Antidepressant drugs and
antianxiety drugs are used more than
tranquilizers because these drugs are
not habit forming. Some people need
to take drugs long term; others only
take them temporarily.
Doctors usually combine cognitive
therapy with medication. The goal is
to help the person recover and
function normally again. If you know
a person who experiences severe panic
attacks or agoraphobia please urge
him or her to consult a doctor. Help is
available.

Answers to item 1 will vary but might
include
1. Agoraphobia is an anxiety disorder;
when a person has it he or she is
afraid to be outside in open places
or in crowds of people.

Answers to items 2–4
2. No, because he or she hates to be in
crowds of people or outside in open
places.
3. A doctor might treat this anxiety
disorder with medication or talking
therapy (counseling).
4. Claustrophobia is a fear of small,
closed places.
Acrophobia is a fear of heights.
Possible other phobias:
Hydrophobia is a fear of water.

Exercise 10 (p. 119)
Answers will vary.

Review Unit 2

I. (p. 120)
  A. 3, 4, 1
  B. 4, 1, 3
  C. 5, 4, 2

II. (p. 120)
  A. 4, 3, 2
  B. 1, 2, 4

III. (p. 121)
  1. f
  2. h
  3. a
  4. g
  5. b
  6. c
  7. d
  8. e

IV. (p. 121)
  1. b
  2. d
  3. f
  4. a
  5. e

V. (p. 122)
  1. huge
  2. city
  3. mind
  4. choice
  5. ill

VI. (p. 122)
  1. overlapped
  2. Sociology
  3. financial
  4. concept
  5. muscle

Unit 7: Georgia O'Keeffe

Vocabulary Preview

Preview 1 (p. 124)
  1. superior
  2. elements
  3. create
  4. method
  5. abstraction

Preview 2 (p. 124)
  1. d
  2. e
  3. b
  4. a
  5. c

Reading Preview (p. 125)

  1. c
  2. b
  3. d

Comprehension Check (p. 130)

  1. F
  2. T
  3. T
  4. T
  5. F
  6. F
  7. F

Exercise 1 (p. 131)
  1. unaware   definition: not aware, not conscious of . . .
  2. uncritical   definition: not judgmental or critical
  3. inexpert   definition: not good at . . . , not professional
  4. infertile   definition: (soil that) does not produce crops; unable to bear children
  5. unreliable   definition: cannot be relied on, not dependable

Exercise 2 (p. 132)
  words: abstraction, visualization, fertility, fertilization, conformity, confrontation, devotion
  1. confrontation
  2. devotion
  3. Fertility
  4. visualization
  5. conformity

Exercise 3 (p. 132)
  1. wealth
  2. pregnant
  3. emotion
  4. cover
  5. equal

6. group
7. culture
8. question
9. method

Exercise 4 (p. 133)
1. b
2. b
3. c
4. a
5. b
6. c
7. a
8. b

Exercise 5 (p. 134)
1. enabled
2. create
3. represent
4. violent
5. female
6. emphasize
7. false
8. distinctive

Exercise 6 (p. 134)
1. enriched
2. individual
3. visual
4. fertile
5. sketches
6. revealed

Exercise 7 (p. 135)
1. production method
2. basic theory, basic design, basic method, basic element, basic product, basic idea
3. sophisticated theory, sophisticated design, sophisticated method, sophisticated product, sophisticated idea
4. scientific theory, scientific method, scientific idea
5. abstract theory, abstract design, abstract idea
6. visual element, visual arts
7. fertile land
8. superior theory, superior design, superior method, superior product, superior idea

Exercise 8 (p. 136)
Answers will vary.
1. sketch: an idea, a plan, a picture   others: a paper, a book
2. reveal: a secret, the meaning, a plan   others: an answer, a clue
3. criticize: a policy, an idea, a picture   others: a person, a (political) party
4. design: a plan, a product, a building   others: a CD cover, a room interior

Exercise 9 (p. 137)
Answers will vary.
Sample answers:
1. Georgia was shocked when doctors and tests showed that she was losing her sight. This happened in 1971, when she was 84.
2. Georgia had had very good vision and had tried to keep it by doing special exercises.
3. Georgia met a potter named Juan Hamilton after she started to go blind. She liked his artwork because it was like hers and told him to concentrate on it.
4. Hamilton taught Georgia how to make pots, which she could do by touch rather than sight. Making pottery made Georgia feel more creative, and she started painting again.

Exercise 10 (p. 137)
Answers will vary.

Exercise 11 (p. 137)
Answers will vary.

Exercise 12 (p. 138)
(1) When I ask students, "What is the strongest element in a painting?" the usual answers are superior technical ability, a strong design, and an individual artistic style. Students never think of the simplest element of all—leaving white paper white. A

little investigation will <u>reveal</u> that the eye quickly picks out shapes of plain white paper. Areas left white reflect light or "glow" more than dark or heavily painted areas which do not reflect much light. As a result, your eye will go to these glowing light areas first.

(2) Because of this luminous, glowing quality, white paper has the same <u>visual</u> power as a heavy, dark color. To understand this idea, try a simple experiment. Paint a black circle in a white square or <u>rectangle</u>. Next to that, paint another square but reverse the colors: paint a white circle within a black square. (It is important to keep both circles the same size in order to compare them fairly!) Now, notice how the white circle appears to expand. Also, notice how your eye is drawn to the white circle more than the black one.

(3) When you create a design the white shapes in it must function as part of the painting. I suggest that you draw out your ideas on <u>sketch</u> paper. Draw the white, unpainted areas as well as the painted ones. Then paint all of the areas of the sketch that will be white in the final painting with *black* paint. This <u>method</u> will give you an "X-ray" of your design that can help you see where it may be unbalanced or weak. When you are finished painting, step back and look <u>critically</u> at the black and white shapes. Are they strong? Does each shape <u>enrich</u> the overall design?

1. picks out
2. expands
3. function as

Exercise 13 (p. 139)
   Answers will vary.
   Sample outline:
   1. Georgia prepares to paint.
      a. She stretches canvas.

   b. She paints canvases with a white undercoat.
   c. She waits for a design to form in her mind.
2. Georgia paints.
   a. She makes a sketch.
   b. She mixes her paints and puts them on her palette.
   c. She paints quickly, only stopping to eat.
   d. She finishes a small painting in one day.
3. About Georgia's paintings
   a. done in a series
   b. She simplifies the object so it does not look realistic.
   c. She selects, eliminates, and emphasizes things to reveal the meaning.
   d. The last picture in a series shows her abstract idea of the essence of the thing she has painted.

Exercise 14 (p. 140)
   Reviews will vary.

Unit 8: Carl Sagan

Vocabulary Preview

Preview 1 (p. 142)
   1. diagram
   2. reactions
   3. planets
   4. technology
   5. constructed

Preview 2 (p. 142)
   1. c
   2. e
   3. b
   4. a
   5. d

Reading Preview (p. 143)
   1. d
   2. c
   3. c
   4. b

Comprehension Check (p. 150)

1. T
2. F
3. T
4. F
5. T
6. T
7. F
8. T
9. F
10. F

Exercise 1 (p. 151)
Extraterrestrial means related to outside or beyond the Earth.
1. b
2. c
3. d
4. a

Exercise 2 (p. 152)
1. biology, meaning: the study or knowledge of living things
2. technology, meaning: the practical application of knowledge
3. astrology, meaning: knowledge of how the positions of the stars and planets will supposedly influence events on Earth
4. psychology, meaning: knowledge about the way the human mind works
5. sociology, meaning: the study of the behavior of groups of people

Exercise 3 (p. 152)
1. C, reason: definition 3 fits this context; to display or show
2. B, reason: this refers to a housing development, a place where people live
3. C, reason: definition 1 fits this context; an estimate of future sales
4. A, reason: definitions 1 and 3 fit this context; it was an idea that was carefully thought out
5. C, reason: definition 2 fits this context; to stick out

Exercise 4 (p. 153)
1. biological
2. technology
3. astronaut
4. psychology
5. Social

Exercise 5 (p. 154)
1. c
2. b
3. a
4. b
5. a
6. c
7. b
8. a

Exercise 6 (p. 154)
1. I, change *environment* to *environmental*
2. C
3. I, change *contract* to *contact*
4. C
5. I, change *principals* to *principles*

Exercise 7 (p. 155)
1. vision of
2. desire to
3. ability to
4. formula for
5. communicate with
6. diagram of
7. in relation to
8. complain about
9. respond to
10. refer to

Exercise 8 (p. 155)
1. Public reaction ~~about~~ the *to* drawings was minimal.
2. OK
3. When called on, the student responded ~~about~~ the correct *with* answer.
4. The young actor had a strong desire ~~of~~ money and fame. *for*

5. The formula ~~on~~ *for, of* the chemical
   ^
   compound is in your textbook.
6. Their vision ~~to~~ *of* the future did not
   ^
   include poor people.
7. Roberto's ~~pitch ability to~~ *pitching ability* was
   ^
   tremendous.
8. OK
9. Who is that man in relation ~~of~~ *to*
   ^
   you? Is he your uncle?
10. This diagram ~~for~~ *of* the planets
    ^
    explains our solar system.

Exercise 9 (p. 156)
   Answers will vary.

Exercise 10 (p. 157)
1. The purpose of the Pioneer 10 mission was to explore the area around Jupiter. Yes, the mission was successful; the ship made it to Jupiter and took the first close-up photographs and measurements of Jupiter.
2. The Pioneer 10 took close-up photos and measurements of Jupiter, was the first ship to use a planet's own gravity to push it into space (a method that is still used today), and showed that our solar system was much bigger than scientists had previously thought.
   Second part: individual responses will vary.
3. Interstellar means *among or between the stars.*
4. For Sagan, the unofficial mission had to do with the plaque. He hoped that the plaque would make us think of ourselves as being a small part of a huge universe. He also hoped that the plaque would someday reach other beings, but he knew this was unlikely.

Exercise 11 (p. 158)
   Essays will vary.

Writing for Different Discourse Communities (p. 159)
   Answers may include, but are not limited to
   humanities (including literature, languages, history, and philosophy)
   arts (including fine arts, music, theater, and dance)
   sciences (chemistry, physics, biology, earth sciences, astronomy, and medicine)
   social sciences (psychology, sociology, and anthropology)
   law
   education

Exercise 12 (p. 159)
   Sample answers:
   a.   Astronomy was interesting this week because it was about Carl Sagan, the only astronomer I ever heard of before this course. Have you gotten to him yet? He was the one in those Nova shows where he went around in a space ship that took you to all parts of the universe. That show was where I first saw a galaxy. I can't remember the name of it now, but it was this beautiful galaxy in all these colors—yellow, blue, white—and I think I fell in love with astronomy right then and there. I was sad to read, though, that Sagan had died. I didn't know that? Did you?
   I'm sorry to say that I missed a class this week. Do you think I could borrow your lecture notes? I had to go to the IS office to get papers for a new student visa and this guy gave me such a bad time. He was this weird guy with a funny way of speaking English and I couldn't understand him at all! Ugh . . . what a waste of time. I'll have to go back on Monday. Hope I can find someone who speaks my kind of English.

b. Carl Sagan gives two main reasons for wanting to popularize science. First, he wanted everyone to feel the wonder and magic of science as he did. He wanted young people, especially, to become interested in how things work in their environment. He also hoped they would be captivated by the idea of a journey of exploration beyond our planet.

Second, Sagan wanted everyone to become involved in saving the planet. He felt that the universe could either be saved through mankind's increased awareness of new discoveries in science and new developments in technology or destroyed through our ignorance and neglect.

Unit 9: Colin Powell

Vocabulary Preview

Preview 1 (p. 162)
1. Allied
2. team
3. reliable
4. rigorous
5. commit

Preview 2 (p. 162)
1. c
2. a
3. e
4. d
5. b

Reading Preview (p. 163)
1. b
2. c
3. d

Comprehension Check (p. 169)
1. F
2. T
3. F
4. T
5. F
6. F
7. F
8. T

Exercise 1 (p. 171)
1. confrontation
2. contract
3. convened
4. congregation
5. consensus
6. conform
7. consult
8. contacted

Exercise 2 (p. 172)
1. rely
2. depend on
3. un-
4. not
5. -able
6. can do something
7. count on, depend
8. unreliable, undependable
9. An unreliable person is someone who cannot be trusted or depended on.

Exercise 3 (p. 172)
1. challenge
2. to dare, to oppose
3. -er
4. one who
5. opponent, rival, competitor
6. teammate, collaborator
7. A challenger is someone who dares to oppose or confront someone.

Exercise 4 (p. 173)
1. person
2. ignorant
3. luxury
4. wish
5. rebel
6. amateur
7. unclear
8. careless

Exercise 5 (p. 173)
1. eloquent speech, eloquent gesture, eloquent speaker, eloquent leader
2. team spirit, team leader
3. allied forces, allied operations
4. task force
5. military spirit, military force, military forces, military weapons

Exercise 6 (p. 174)
1. assembled
2. rely
3. Military
4. devotions
5. dedicated
6. committed

Exercise 7 (p. 175)

Military Terms				
People	Event	Equipment	Rank	Organizational Unit
airmen	Desert	tankers	sergeant	platoon
GI	Storm	P-51	general	First Armored
general	Gulf War	aircraft	chairman	Division
sergeant			of the	tank company
defense			Joint	VII Corps
contractor			Chiefs	
military			of	
leaders			Staff	

Exercise 8 (p. 175)
1. a
2. a
3. c
4. b
5. a
6. c
7. b
8. a

Exercise 9 (p. 176)
1. b
2. a
3. c
4. c
5. a

Exercise 10 (p. 178)
Answers will vary.

Exercise 11 (p. 178)
Answers will vary.

Exercise 12 (p. 179)

Plato's Ideal Society

Preeminent among the Greeks of the fifth century B.C. was Plato, the Athenian philosopher who is best remembered today for *The Republic*, the dialogue in which he presents an eloquent vision of the ideal society. *The Republic* is primarily dedicated to Plato's notion that only the wise should rule. Plato was against the idea that men should rule just because they had proven to be powerful military leaders. All one had to do, Plato pointed out, was to look at what Pericles, a renowned general and statesman of Athens, had done for his people. True, he had devoted much of his energy to the beautification of Athens, but he had also plunged his beloved city-state into a disastrous war that had ultimately led to its downfall.

The challenge facing every man, Plato argued, was to search for eternal wisdom. Only those who dedicated many years of their lives to considering eternal questions such as What is truth? What is honor? What is justice? ultimately arrived at wisdom and were then qualified to become philosopher-kings.

Many people are not aware of the fact that Plato was one of our first feminists. Unlike almost every other well-known thinker of his time, Plato held that women could become as wise as men and thus could also be relied upon to provide wise guardianship.

But what about the rest of the people; what was their role to be in Plato's ideal society? Well, those who were spirited, courageous, and interested in honor and glory were to become the protectors and defenders of the state. The rest, the common people, were to be laborers whose task it would be to employ whatever special gift or ability they had for the benefit of the state.

And what if some of these common people refused to conform to what the state dictated for them? Well, said Plato, they would have to be taught the value of working for the common good.

Exercise 13 (p. 180)
    Answers will vary.

Review Unit 3

I. (p. 181)
   A. 3, 4, 2
   B. 5, 2, 3
   C. 3, 5, 2

II. (p. 181)
   1. repair
   2. lie
   3. geology
   4. method
   5. finance

III. (p. 182)
   1. c
   2. e
   3. a
   4. f
   5. b

IV. (p. 182)
   1. nonviolent
   2. biology
   3. misunderstand
   4. transform
   5. fertility
   6. creator

V. (p. 182)
   1. d
   2. e
   3. a
   4. b
   5. g
   6. h
   7. c

VI. (p. 183)
   1. illustrations
   2. generated
   3. option
   4. solar
   5. eloquent

How to Make Your Own Vocabulary Word Index Cards and Vocabulary Notebook

1. Write the following words on cards, approximately business card size.
2. On the back of each card write the meaning or meanings of the word in your native language. If it's helpful to you, write the phonetic pronunciation of the word and a sample sentence containing the word.
3. Practice with these cards when you have time. Look at the word on the front. Try to remember the meaning of the word. Check the back of the card to see if you are correct. Retest yourself on the cards you miss.
4. Review the vocabulary cards periodically. This will help you remember and master these words.
5. In addition to making vocabulary word index cards, you may want to make your own vocabulary notebook. If you read or hear a word you do not know, consult your dictionary for the meaning of the word. Write this in a vocabulary notebook. If it's helpful to you, write the phonetic pronunciation of the word and a sample sentence containing the word. By the time you finish the notebook, you will have your own academic learner dictionary.

abstract	assign	community
accomplish	assist	complex
adapt	attain	complicate
adjust	automatic	component
alcohol	available	comprehend
allied	aware	conceive
approach	career	concentrate
appropriate	challenge	concept
arbitrary	commit	conduct
assemble	communicate	conform

construct	feature	reaction
consult	fertile	rectangle
consume	finance	reliable
contact	function	research
contract	generate	reside
controversial	goal	reveal
create	hero	reverse
critic	huge	revolt
crucial	illustrate	rigorous
culture	impression	rotate
decade	income	series
dedicate	individual	site
depress	intellect	sketch
design	intelligent	sociology
devote	interpret	solar
diagram	issues	specify
diameter	layer	statistic
drama	legal	superiority
drug	luxury	supplement
economy	mental	supreme
edit	method	task
element	military	team
eliminate	minimum	technology
eloquent	muscle	terror
embrace	nervous	text
emerge	option	theory
emotion	overlap	tiny
enrich	perpendicular	transform
environment	persist	undertake
establish	planet	urban
evident	primitive	utter
evoke	principle	version
evolve	project	visual
expert	psychology	voluntary
exponent	quote	withdraw